The Authentic Person

DEALING WITH DILEMMA

SYDNEY J. HARRIS

ARGUS COMMUNICATIONS Niles, Illinois 60648

design by PATRICIA ELLEN RICCI

published by ARGUS COMMUNICATIONS,
NILES, ILLINOIS 60648

International Standard Book Number: 0-913592-00-5

Contents

Preface.............................. 5

1. The Dethroning of Man:
   A New Self-Image............... 9

2. Threading Through
   The Semantic Woods............. 21

3. Polarities: Positive Attitudes
   Toward Creative Tension......... 37

4. Morality and
   The Authentic Person........... 61

5. Polarities in Our Social
   and Political Institutions.......... 75

6. The Obsolescence of Dualism
   In a Converging World Community. 95

7. The Personal Paradox:
   The Individual and the Collective...107

8. Modern Man:
   Paradox in Process.............121

Explanation of Terms.............133

Selected Bibliography.............138

PREFACE

In a real sense, this little book "wrote itself" over the years. It began in the early 1950's as a lecture prepared for the Aspen Institute for Humanistic Studies. Gradually, the lecture grew and changed as it was presented to more and different audiences, at colleges, churches, and various symposiums.

What the book tries to do, briefly, is to stimulate thought *about the way we think*, with less emphasis on the subjects we think about and more on the process and the person doing the thinking. If there has been a revolution in philosophy in the late 20th century, it is the realization that the abstract "philosopher" is only a "man thinking"—and that the man is fully as important as the thinking and the object of thought.

By a happy mnemonic coincidence, the three basic ideas I deal with in the book all begin with a "P"—Paradox, Polarity, and Personalism. These three are, in my view, the keys to coping with many of the dilemmas of modern man, and "coping" seems to me a more realistic and realizable goal than "solving." We are still far from the right answers, if there are any—

but perhaps we may begin to ask some of the right questions.

The modest aim of *The Authentic Person* is to look afresh at some old problems and to see whether we have failed to come to grips with them because they are intractable or insoluble, or because hitherto we have failed to ask the right questions. It is an exercise in *thinking about thinking*, which means, inescapably, reconsidering ourselves as Pascal's "thinking reed" in Nature.

The contents of this book are purposely diverse—and may seem to be diffuse—because I have ranged over a broad territory, from morals to musical taste and from marriage to world government in order to demonstrate the inter-connectedness of Paradox, Polarity and Personalism in widely disparate areas. I have chosen these topics not because I pretend to any special competence in them but simply as examples and illustrations, from the most intimate level of our being to the most universal.

After this word of explanation, I feel that a note of apology and general acknowledgment are necessary. Since this book was originally a collection of lecture notes scribbled on cards, it is more than likely that over the years I have forgotten the sources of some of the quotations and passages, which have consequently become imbedded in the text without appropriate attribution.

Pardon is begged in advance from any who may have been so cavalierly treated. In the past thirty years as a writer, my own words have too often been appropriated with a singular disregard for their source. It is not a pleasant feeling to be the victim of plagiarism—however unintended—and I have a heavy awareness of unexpressed debt in the following pages.

I must express my explicit debt, however, to Emmanuel Mounier, the founder of French "personalism" in the journal *Esprit;* to Martin Buber, whose concept of "the narrow ridge" germinated my own view of polarity; and to Reinhold Niebuhr, whose long and patient talks with me at Aspen provided the seedlings from which this book has, finally, sprung.

Sydney J. Harris

Door County, Wisconsin.
August, 1972.

CHAPTER ONE

The Dethroning of Man: A New Self-Image

Do the same problems afflict the same kinds of men throughout history? Or do the problems change, while the men remain much as they ever were? When we discuss "the dilemmas of modern man," what are we *really* talking about?

Most people would agree that problems change: each age poses its own particular set of equations, which the society of that time must master or come to terms with. The sheepherder in a pastoral society, the tallow-maker in a feudal society, the auto mechanic in an industrial society, have had different worlds to face.

But what about the men and women themselves, living in any given time and social order? Are Homer's warriors basically "the same" as American G.I.s slogging through Vietnam? Is Penelope, weaving and waiting for the return of Odysseus, little different from the modern war wife, who may be working in a factory while her husband fights abroad?

A basic question, rarely even asked in philosophy or psychology, is: how do we view ourselves, compared with the ways that people in the past viewed themselves? It is a basic question, for the way we view ourselves determines, in large part, how we feel, think, and react toward the world around us. Our self-estimation is the unit by which we estimate everything else. What we think a man (or woman) is, or ought to be, or was meant to be, shapes our life-styles.

It is one of the three main themes of this book that "modern man" differs radically from even his recent ancestors, and therefore today's problems contain a significant dimension that was lacking in the past. It is the combination of these two differences— *within* us and *outside* us —that gives our age its peculiarly perplexing, threatening, and uncertain quality.

Every era in history, of course, has considered itself "modern," in comparison with the past. But such modernity in the past was mostly a matter of *external* change —new fashions, new artifacts, changing forms of governmental or commercial relations, explorations and inventions and conveniences unknown to one's forebears.

Within the last hundred years, however, three fundamental revolutions have combined to alter radically the *internal* landscape of man (or what Gerard Manley Hopkins so felicitously termed the "inscape"). Man is now qualitatively different from his ancestors for the first time in recorded history—and this qualitative difference implies the need for a new approach to both the perennial and the contemporary dilemmas of mankind.

What is distinctively novel within us is the cumulative result of the three revolutions of the last hundred years—the Darwinian, the Einsteinian, and the Freudian. (There is a fourth, and subsidiary, revolution, the Marxian, which I shall discuss in its proper place.) Together, these revolutions in thought have shaped and reshaped, informed and deformed, man's image of himself. The *self-image* of mankind is distinctively new in the 20th Century—and this self-image is what we may rightfully call "modern man."

The Darwinian revolution changed our relation to the natural world: man was seen to be removed from his special place in the order of creation. His view of nature, and of himself as part of it, underwent a drastic revision.

The Einsteinian revolution changed our relation to the universe. Until then, we had lived in a comfortable Newtonian universe—a kind of gigantic watch factory, with its springs and

11

... Every age thinks of itself
as "modern..."

pendulums, its predictable movements, and its immutable "laws" of mechanical accuracy.

Then, suddenly, the character of the universe changed before our eyes. Time and space were no longer regarded as independent entities, but as parts of one another, as a baffling "time-space continuum." The idea of infinity was challenged; we learned that parallel lines somehow *could* meet in "curved space"; and the distinction between matter and energy, which had seemed so simple and obvious and fundamental to us, was shattered once and for all with Einstein's famous equation, which has given us atomic fission and all the potency and peril attendant upon it.

At about the same time, the Western world began to undergo perhaps the most agonizing revolution of all —the Freudian revolution, from which the patient is still quivering in a state of shock. If Darwin changed our relation to created things and Einstein changed our relation to the physical universe, Freud changed our conscious relation to one another and to ourselves. Post-Freudian man —which all of us are, like it or not, know it or not —can never again think of himself in the same terms as his ancestors thought of themselves.

Although the idea of the unconscious is a very old one in natural philosophy, its extent and its influence had never before been explored and mapped so fully and convincingly. But the Freudian revolution did much more than reveal the unconscious bases of behavior. It also cast a new, harsh, and seemingly pitiless light on ancient questions of morality, of sexuality, of free will and determinism, of the whole structure of social relations.

The therapeutic influence of Freudianism has thus far been relatively small; but its cultural and sociological influence has been immense and pervasive. No area of modern life has been exempt from its scrutiny or has been unaffected by its probings. The enormous contemporary interest in psychology and scrutiny of the "self" — almost unknown to previous generations — is the direct result of Freud's penetrating insights into a hitherto neglected area of man's basic inner needs and drives.

Together, these three revolutions completed the dethroning of man, which was begun when Copernicus demonstrated that our earth is not the center and crown of the universe. This was the first terrible blow to our self-esteem as a species — to learn that the earth was a relatively obscure planet in a small solar system tucked away in an insignificant part of a galaxy that was only one of millions exactly like it.

Thus disappeared the first of man's absolute claims to distinction. Next Darwin showed that we are closer to the apes than to the angels in our origin — that we share a common descent with the other primates. Then Einstein "relativized" the universe, and in so doing paved the way for the general belief that "everything is relative," from musical taste to moral systems. Finally, Freud disabused man of the sovereignty of his "rational" powers by disclosing the strength and persistence of unconscious drives that determine many of the decisions we imagine that we consciously make.

So that these three modern revolutions, while adding enormously to man's intellectual growth, have at the same time come to be regarded as emotional deprivations. They have taken something away from man — his sense of a secure and stable place in the hierarchy of the universe — and what they have replaced it with is still a matter of uneasy speculation.

What has been taken away, in a phrase, is our *identity*. The more we learned about ourselves, the less we thought of ourselves; the acquisition of knowledge was inversely accompanied by the diminishing of identity. Except that we have faith (and understand what faith is, apart from mere ignorance, credulity, or sentimentality), we do not know where we

15

If Darwin changed our
relation to created things, and
Einstein changed our relation to
the physical universe,
Freud changed our relation
to one another and to ourselves.

came from, who we are, what we are doing here, and where, if anywhere, we are going.

Out of a seeming order in the past, we have arrived at disorder at every level; out of a sense of permanence and regularity, we have been reduced to the blind struggle for survival in Darwin's terms, to the statistical swirling of neutrons in Einstein's terms, to the darkly primitive strivings of the irrational in Freud's terms. At least this is what the layman makes of these theories, this is how he feels —even though Darwin, Einstein and Freud themselves might feel (and indeed did feel) quite differently.

Now, if the man in the street knows little about these ideas beyond their names, how then did they come to have such profound influence upon his thoughts and feelings? The mass of uneducated citizens, and even the minority of educated men and women, have only the scantiest conception of social Darwinism, or the special theory of relativity or the workings of the id. Is it conceivable that these scientific abstractions have significantly altered the way men and women regard themselves and their society, or is it only intellectuals who imagine such impact upon the ordinary person?

The Germans, who have a word for everything, have the word *Zeitgeist*, meaning "spirit

17

of the age," that sums up this kind of impact. Through a kind of social and cultural osmosis, a combination of ideas and trends and theories seeps into the public consciousness, permeates into the pores of even those who are unaware of it. And the *Zeitgeist* of the 20th century has consisted chiefly of the Darwinian "survival of the fittest," the Einsteinian "all is relative," and the Freudian "primacy of the irrational."

(It must be interjected here that each of these slogans is a simplification and a vulgarization and, hence, a distortion of the complex and sophisticated theories they represent; but every seminal idea suffers such violation at the hands of its friends as much as its enemies. The tenets of Marxism, in their modern form, have been even more crudely torn from their humanistic roots.)

Beginning at the end of World War I (which some historians say was truly the end of the 19th century and the beginning of the 20th, in a psychological rather than a chronological sense), the worlds of architecture and painting and music and philosophy and literature and communication generally reflected this torn-up feeling and outraged sensibility. All the new "movements," however diverse in substance, signified a bold break with the past; experimentation, innovation, novelty, and total subjectivism were the rallying cries in all the arts.

18

Man, having been dethroned, had to make his own place, create his own meaning, establish his own values — not only artistically but sexually, socially, politically, and philosophically.

CHAPTER TWO

Threading Through
The Semantic Woods

Before the Darwinian, Einsteinian, and Freudian revolutions, men, with few exceptions, had a sense of identity and continuity; identity in the social and personal sense and continuity in the historical and metaphysical sense. Their world was small, compact, and simple. But whether believers or unbelievers, they shared a sense of purpose and meaning. For the most part, they believed in something called progress or providence or salvation, however variously they defined these terms. Leaning heavily on the Greek inheritance, they felt that a faculty called "reason" would eventually dominate in human affairs. They saw life primarily as a struggle between "barbarism" and "civilization" and rarely doubted that Christian or rational man represented the forces of civilization and that these forces were good and would prevail.

Now, what we have inherited from the past have been systems of thought or belief which, however they differed in content, were all based on some sort of *Dualism*. Before these three revolutions, men conceived the world and themselves in terms of permanent and irreconcilable *Opposites*. Philosophically, there was Realism on one side and Idealism on the other. Psychologically, there was Love at one end of the spectrum of emotions and Hate at the other end. Physically, there was Matter, which was visible and palpable, and Spirit, which was not.

Even though Christianity officially conquered the Gnostic heresy as early as the 4th century, most of the Western world continued — and continues — to believe in this duality of opposites. (The Gnostics divided the cosmos into the forces of Light and Dark, or Good and Evil, or Spiritual and Material, perpetually contending for victory against each other. Christianity, with its roots deep in Judaism, refused to accept the notion that the created world of matter was intrinsically "bad." In this basic sense, Christianity and Judaism are not "spiritual" religions, like those of the East.)

The dilemmas of modern man are mainly caused, in my opinion, by the fact that his entire mode of thinking and feeling and speaking and acting has been conditioned by this duality. This is the key, I truly believe, to many of the central problems that baffle and frustrate us in our attempts to come to grips with the strange, frightening, contradictory, unstable 20th century.

For the new world of the 20th century is a world of *Paradox;* and it cannot be dealt with, or even comprehended, as though it were a world of Duality. When we try to do so, we become impaled on both horns of our dilemma. Yet almost all our thinking today — or what passes for thinking, even in trained academic circles — is based upon this outmoded duality.

Before I offer some specific examples of duality, it is first necessary to take the reader back to his freshman course in formal logic for a moment and review the difference between the words *contrary* and *contradictory*. This will be enormously helpful in threading our way through the semantic woods and arriving at a common agreement about the words we are using.

Contrary statements are statements like "This paper is green" and "This paper is red." If one statement is true, the other must be false; they cannot both be true at the same time. But — and this is crucial — *they can both be false together:* the paper might be neither green nor red, but white.

Contradictory statements are statements like "This paper is green" and "This paper is not green." If one statement is true, the other is false; if one statement is false, the other is true. Unlike contraries, contradictories cannot

Zeitgeist

The germans, who
have a word for everything,
have the word Zeitgeist,
meaning "spirit of the age,"
that sums up this kind
of impact.

be false together. The truth or falsity of one determines the truth or falsity of the other.

A failure to recognize this elementary logical difference can result in our supposing that two conflicting viewpoints are contradictory when they are merely contrary, and arguing that one or the other must prevail. This kind of false Dualism is most dramatically illustrated in the rivalry between adherents of Communism and the Competitive Individual Society, as Capitalism likes to style itself.

Both we and the Russians (or Chinese or Cubans) assume that we have contradictory systems and that if one is proved "right" the other is proved "wrong", or vice versa. In actuality, no such contradiction exists: we have contrary systems, or polarities, and it is entirely possible that some third system, combining the better elements of each, might be superior to either Communism or Capitalism.

The reason we get so confused on this question is that Dictatorship and Democracy are true contradictories; you can have one or the other, but not a combination of both. Dictatorship and Democracy, however, are political concepts, whereas Communism and Capitalism are economic ones. There is a scale leading from "pure" communism to "pure" capitalism (needless to say, neither of them exists anywhere in its pure state), and we can stop any-where we decide to on that scale. Communism and Capitalism are polarities, or contraries, while Dictatorship and Democracy are genuine opposites, or dualities.

There is no inherent reason for Capitalism to be accompanied by democracy, any more than for Communism to be accompanied by dictatorship. Spain has capitalism and dicta-torship; Sweden has socialism (a moderate form of Communism) along with democracy. Fascism combines elements of capitalism and socialism (it was no accident that Hitler called his party the National Socialist German Work-ers' Party) and what is called communism in the Soviet Union is really state capitalism.

People are confused by these terms and en-gage in fruitless arguments because they have not carefully analyzed the nature of contraries and contradictories. Most people think in terms of black-and-white, of either-or, and fail to discriminate among categories of thought.

Now let me make another distinction, as I did between "contraries" and "contradictor-ies." This one is between "duality" and "polar-ity," and is even more important than the for-mer distinction.

A duality is fundamentally a contradiction that cannot be brought into alliance with its

26

opposite. War and peace are such a duality; you cannot have a "little war" in a community and still have civil peace. Virginity and sexual experience are a duality; the semi-virgin exists only in the remote regions of romantic fiction.

Many persons would insist that freedom and security are likewise a duality, but they would be wrong. Freedom and security are a polarity, and there is a world of difference between a polarity and a duality. It is absolutely crucial to understand this before we begin to examine political or social problems.

First think of these terms in a psychological, or emotional, sense: it is the feeling of emotional security that gives us genuine freedom, and it is the freedom to express our inner selves that gives us an abiding sense of security. The two complement, or *contreplete*, one another in a kind of creative tension, like a tightrope wire that is neither too tight nor too loose.

As the Freudians have shown, the person who lacks emotional security (as all neurotics do) has no real freedom to act in certain areas. Some of his behavior is compulsive, repetitive, and responsive to past conditioning rather than to the reality of the present.

Genuine freedom in personal and social relationships comes from a deep sense of security

...in marriage, as in society generally, we find that the polarities of Freedom and Security are false opposites -- for a secure marriage provides freedom, and the freedom of expression gives us a sense of security.

—knowing who we are, where we belong, and what is expected of us. The neurotic, lacking this sense of security, is unfree, bound to his infantile needs and unconscious drives. He does not "act" as much as he "reacts" to people and situations, and such reaction is usually predetermined by his early emotional crippling.

Conversely, without some measure of freedom, there is no real security. The slave is the least secure of all men because he can be bought today and sold tomorrow; he has no control over his own destiny. People who live in despotic or dictatorial societies have no true security—even though the despot or the state may provide everything they need—because they lack the freedom to make choices.

And this is the heart of the polarity—freedom depends on the ability to make choices. Without choice, there is no freedom. A starving person will take any job that is offered him; he will eat any food that is thrown his way. In order to exercise a meaningful freedom—which is a social relation, and not a personal attribute—a human being must have viable options for action with or against others. A hermit is neither free nor unfree.

The same is true for society as for the individual. Freedom in a social sense cannot mean freedom to starve or go without a job when a man is willing and able to work. A man faced with running into a mine field or a burning building has no significant freedom, for the consequences of both options are equally fatal. The "most freedom" must mean, then, having the widest possible selection of alternatives to choose from.

This is precisely where the essential polarity of security comes in. Only a person whose existence rests on a minimal base of security can exercise freedom. Only when the stomach is full can the mind make voluntary decisions. Only when a man's job or family or life itself does not depend upon force or fate or caprice is he then truly free to make a fully human decision.

In a just social order, the polarities of freedom and security are kept in equilibrium, and there is enough freedom to reward exceptional talent, merit, or enterprise but also enough security to give people free and rational choices. What good is freedom in the abstract if realistic conditions tie a person to a treadmill from which there is no hope of release?

In the collectivist societies, such as the Soviet Union, the balance is tipped in favor of security at the expense of freedom; in the capitalistic countries, such as the U.S., the balance is tipped in favor of freedom at the expense of security. The irony of this antipodal situation is that the Russians cannot achieve equilibrium until they reach the security of freedom; and we cannot achieve equilibrium until we reach the freedom of security. In both nations, the "wire" is too loose or too tight for the optimum of rope-walking.

It is notable that, in recent years, both nations have been moving tentatively toward equilibrium: the Soviet Union is experimenting with a market economy, and the U.S. is expanding its welfare policies. Both these ventures serve to demonstrate the truth that freedom and security are necessary complements to each other, and not opposites, or contradictories.

On a more personal level, people still talk about the Flesh and the Spirit as though they were opposed and fixed entities. But this is not at all the case. Advances in psychosomatic medicine have taught us that the body and the psyche are totally interrelated, that they act and react upon one another. Man is not a dualism of body and mind but an organism in which mental attitudes affect the body and bodily functions affect the mind.

What Smuts called "the holistic approach" — the approach to the person not as a "patient"

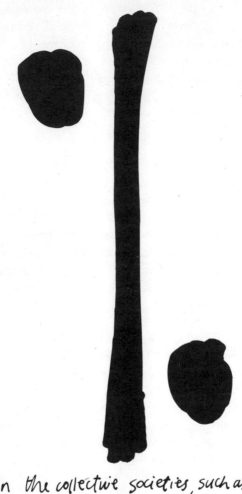

In the collective societies, such as Russia,
the balance is tipped in favor of security
at the expense of freedom; in the
capitalistic countries, such as the U.S.,
the balance is tipped in favor of
freedom at the expense of security ....

or a set of symptoms, but as a whole person — is more and more coming to the fore in the practice of modern medicine and psychotherapy. As Osler said: "It is not so much the kind of disease a person gets as the kind of person who gets the disease," that is engaging the attention of medical science. The Spirit and the Flesh are polarities that sustain each other, not dualities that ignore or oppose each other.

Consider the polarities of Love and Hate, which in the past have been thought of as dualities. We have learned, somewhat to our dismay at first, that rather than being opposites, they contain and sometimes even embrace each other. There is no love without a tinge of hate and no hate without at least a trace of attraction. As numerous theologians have noted, the true opposite of love is indifference.

The lacerations that are sometimes made public in the divorce courts offer proof, if proof is still needed, that people who were once in love, or thought they were, have residues of the fiercest hatred toward each other. Experienced lawyers agree that no adversaries in court are nearly so angry, spiteful, or vindictive as the average divorcing couple.

When what has long been considered to be a duality is revealed as a polarity, we have a

33

The sweetness needs salt for taste,
the light needs the darkness for
contrast, the individual needs
the society, the pursuit of
competition requires the restraint
of cooperation, the masculine
personality in men must be
tempered by some feminine traits,
just as the feminine personality
must be endowed with some masculine
traits, or both become monsters and
not human beings.

paradoxical situation — seemingly self-contradictory, but true.

CHAPTER THREE

Polarities: Positive Attitudes Toward Creative Tension

Since we have just been in the divorce courts, however briefly, let me provide an illustration of paradox in that most familiar and yet most mysterious relationship — marriage. A marriage is first of all a paradox, and it cannot be understood or lived with until this fact is first grasped by the heart as well as by the mind.

A marriage is an interdependence of two personalities who are joined together for a common purpose: to make a home, and, if possible and desirable, to rear children. In this literal, Old Testament sense, marriage is a *bondage*. Yet it must also be a *freedom* — and this is the heart of the paradox.

In marriage, the man and the woman are independent, but they must also be interdependent. One must not be always dominant and the other always subordinate; one must not sacrifice his or her individuality to the needs of the other. In such cases, I think we will agree,

37

we have a pathological relationship in which sick, neurotic needs are being served on both sides. Or, as someone has described such marriages, inelegantly but accurately: "The rocks in his head perfectly fit the holes in hers."

In what we would commonly (if loosely) call a "good" marriage, each partner is free to grow, to develop, to cultivate his or her own tastes, to be sometimes dominant and sometimes subservient, to find in the security of marriage a freedom hardly possible in any other relationship. (Thus in marriage, as in society generally, we find that freedom and security are polarities and not false opposites, for a secure marriage provides freedom, and the freedom of expression gives us a sense of security.)

Why should this paradox be so? Mainly, because man himself is a paradoxical creature in his deepest needs and demands.

As Paul Tillich, that keen student of existential paradox, has observed: "What is most characteristically *human* about us is the tension between the desire to be 'free' — self-identifying and self-choosing — and to be 'related' — to love and be loved."

If this be true, and I am sure it is, then what should be the basic attitude in a marriage that is meant to endure? It is the willingness *to withstand the tension between the polarities.*

Faced with tension, the instinctive reaction of the human animal, like most animals, is one of two behaviors — fight or flight. This is true, of course, in marriage. When friction reaches a certain point, the tendency is to let it erupt in a fight — which may clear the air, but usually resolves nothing, for most fights center on *symptoms* and not on *causes* — or else to flee the scene: the man grabs his hat and makes for a friend, a bar, or a club, and the woman flies to mother or some surrogate mother-figure.

The ability to sustain a marriage — because even a so-called "good" one is a hard one — consists in the ability to maintain this tension without fight or flight, to work it out or to let it work itself out. Perhaps no one is stable or mature enough to do this all the time — sporadically, we all retreat to childhood when crossed or frustrated — but certainly the rational goal to aim at is the maintenance of the tension between polarities.

Now I suggest that maintaining the tension between seeming "opposites" is the chief way to cope with most of our dilemmas in the modern world. And this is just about the hardest attitude imaginable for a race of beings conditioned for millennia to swing to one opposite or the other, to view life as an immutable dualism between the "good" (my way) and the "bad" (your way).

It is important here that I interject a note of warning against misinterpretation. Maintaining a tension between polarities is not the same as following "the golden mean." It is not the same as taking a middle-of-the-road position. It is not the same as saying that we must always avoid extremes. (Socrates, after all, took an "extreme" position when he refused to escape from prison and decided to accept the hemlock.) Sometimes, as Louis W. Norris remarks in his excellent and sadly-neglected book *Polarity*, there can be such a thing as a "golden extreme."

Adopting a middle-of-the-road position is usually just tepidity and timidity, but to grasp a paradox and to hold it in tension, requires courage and wisdom.

What is the actual practical difference between simply taking a middle view and holding polarities in tension? If we merely follow the middle of the road, we have no rational position, for historically, the road keeps turning and winding, sometimes to the left, sometimes to the right. If our main purpose is to stay in the middle, our position is determined not by our own independent thinking, but by the political and social geography of our times.

Holding the polarities in tension means finding the optimum point at which they work together best; and this is not necessarily in the middle. For instance, the polarities of "permissiveness" and "discipline" may be different for each child or each culture. Some children respond best to a maximum of permissiveness, and others need a tight rein. Each polarity should be given its fullest expression, when the situation or the need calls for it; but the equation must be based on the object to be attained, not on some abstract dogmatic formula.

In making what Norris has happily called "a calculus for polarity," we do not deny or dilute either position; instead, we keep our eye on the particular, immediate goal and try to calculate the best method of attaining it — even if it may turn out, in some cases, to be an "extreme" method. However, we judge things as particulars and not as abstract universals, just as we must judge persons individually, and not as members of some abstract collection.

(In passing, what is wrong with most extremism in political action, for instance, is that political extremists are incapable by temperament of holding any tension between polarities. Indeed, the tension is the very thing they find intolerable, and they seek to snap it

Holding the polarities
in tension means finding
the optimum point at which
they work together best; and
this is not necessarily at the 'center.

by providing oversimplified, black-and-white answers that usually raise more problems than they solve.)

This tension I speak of may be described, in Nietzsche's famous metaphor, as a tightrope over an abyss, which man must walk across to meet his destiny. If the rope is too slack, he will fall; if it is too tight, it has no resiliency, and he will also fall. So the rope must be continually adjusted and supported at its weakest point, wherever that may happen to be.

Modern architecture is following something of the same kind of dynamics in building structures (such as Buckminster Fuller's Dymaxion House) that depend upon opposite stresses contrepleting each other, so that the elements reinforce rather than rest upon one another in a pattern of mutual tension that provides far more strength and flexibility than conventional structures. A dome constructed on this principle could be built over an entire city. Such a project would be physically impossible using traditional concepts of architecture. Fuller uses polarities of "stress" to sustain each other at the optimum points of tensile strength for each — a radically modern concept in building.

Let me give another example of polarity that transforms into paradox. On a gray, bleak day, I walk down a crowded downtown street and look at the faces passing me, and I feel that the public is truly a rabble — ignorant, prejudiced, incompetent, unattractive, stupid, slothful, inconsiderate, incapable of governing themselves with the kind of excellence that Jefferson envisioned for a democratic society.

Then, on another day, a lovely summer afternoon, the very same faces seem vital and warm, repositories of good will, sharing with me a common hope and dream, endowed with a native shrewdness and sense of values, and filled with the potentialities for realizing the hope of Jefferson and his colleagues.

Now it seems to me that both views are right and both are wrong, at the same time and in the same way. And this is the paradox at the heart of the commonweal. The false aristocrat sees the people only in the shadow of the gray day; the false liberal sees them bathed only in the sentimental radiance of the sunny day.

What neither of them is capable of doing — and what is so really hard to do — is to hold both these concepts in tension at once, to recognize that both are right and both are wrong, depending upon what one is asking of people, on what one is trying to do *with* them, or *for* them, or *against* them.

People are stupid; they are also shrewd. As the number of people in any group increases, the average intelligence quotient goes down; but at the same time, the average level of judgment goes up. People are kind, cruel, generous and selfish. What we call human nature is like a vast organ, capable of the deepest or highest tones, of magnificent harmonies or ear-splitting cacophonies.

Learning to regard the same phenomenon in different lights is an attitude, by the way, that scientists have become quite familiar with. The world of subatomic physics is filled with paradoxes, with seeming contradictions held at the same time. Science, as you know, has two theories of light: one is that light is a corpuscle, the other that light is a wave. In developing an equation or an experiment, scientists sometimes employ the corpuscular theory; at other times, they employ the wave theory. Both are "true" operationally, yet logically, they are incompatible with each other.

Scientists have come to accept and to live with this kind of ambiguity; but the matter-of-fact layman is reluctant to adopt the same attitude, perhaps for fear of being thought inconsistent or self-contradictory. Yet if we were willing to hold differing views in tandem, as it were, the duality of thinking in our civic and political life might not be so vicious, so intransigent, and so fruitless.

William James made an observation that goes to the heart of this problem. James wrote: "An unlearned carpenter of my acquaintance once said in my hearing, 'There is very little difference between one man and another; but what little there is, is very important.'"

How admirably, James remarked, this untutored carpenter was able to hold these two ideas in productive tension. We must never forget for a moment how small the differences are between men, or we become snobs and bigots and worse. At the same time, we must not forget for a moment how very important those small differences are, or we encourage mediocrity and a false egalitarian spirit that reduces men to their lowest common denominator.

A social dilemma that vexes us greatly these days is the shifting relationship between what is "moral" and what is "psychological." Society used to treat mentally sick people as if they were evil, or possessed of demons; today we have almost swung to the other extreme, and we tend to regard "bad" people as mentally sick.

It is easy to see, of course, that our ancestors were ignorantly wrong in reproaching or punishing the mentally disturbed as though they were justly suffering for some sins they had committed. On the other hand, if all anti-social conduct is mentally sick, then free will and responsibility can no longer be regarded as human categories, and the moral sphere becomes subordinate to the psychological sphere.

In past ages, the church tended to usurp the functions of the scientist and the doctor (who, admittedly, could do little to help patients) with generally disastrous results. But the contrary of a bad thing is not necessarily a good thing, and labeling people whose behavior we disapprove of as "mad" or "psychotic" may be no improvement over labeling them "wicked" or "sinners." (The despotism of a priestly caste remains despotism, whether the despot wears a surplice or a clinical smock.)

I suggest that the problem is insoluble if we adopt either viewpoint exclusively. There is a moral realm and there is a psychological realm, just as light behaves sometimes as corpuscles and sometimes as waves. It is the operation we are trying to perform that should determine how we regard the acts of certain people. Some persons require incarceration and some require treatment; some acts are bad, some acts are sick, and many acts are a combination of both.

Adopting a middle-of-the-road position is usually just tepidity and timidity -- but to grasp a paradox and to hold it in tension, requires courage and wisdom.

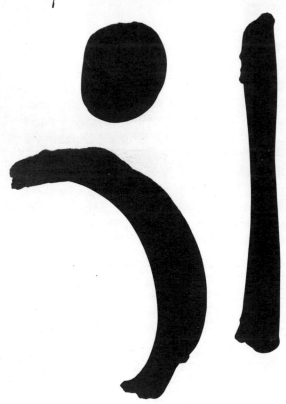

Unless we can hold these concepts in a sophisticated tension, refusing to be pulled one way or the other by doctrinaire considerations, we shall be perpetually arguing about the matter in a dualistic way and getting absolutely nowhere.

(It is interesting to note, in this connection, that recently the Soviet Union has committed some poets and intellectuals to mental institutions rather than to prisons as in the past, on the presumptive grounds that someone must be "crazy" to oppose the government.)

The question of morality touches on perhaps the most important and severe of all modern dilemmas -- which is the widespread division, on all fronts, between the Moral Absolutists and the Moral Relativists. Everybody living leans toward one or the other, whether or not he has ever heard of these terms or understands what they refer to.

The moral absolutist — a shrinking band in modern times — holds that "good" and "evil" are objective terms, that the same standards of conduct apply to all men at all times in all societies. All religious organizations are morally absolutist, in one way or another, for they all hold that their tenets are universally applicable.

The moral relativist — which, I would estimate, includes ninety percent of modern

Western man, even those who nominally belong to churches —holds that "good" and "evil" are relative terms, depending on the society, the time, and the point of view. He holds that most of what we call "morality" is not God-given but man-made, is conventional, arbitrary, culture-bound, and often downright false. He points to differing customs, to changing mores, and to the absurdities of past legislation and ecclesiastical edicts of what is moral and what is not.

If the differences between moral absolutists and moral relativists were merely philosophical ones, it would not matter so much, but the way we conceptualize the nature of morality has practical, immediate, and long-lasting consequences. What we think about right and wrong determines how we act and react in many crucial life situations.

I have studied this question earnestly, and as deeply as I know how for some twenty-five years, and it is my absolute belief that both positions are relatively true. I suppose that makes me a "relative absolutist," but I'll carry the foolish and paradoxical title gladly.

What I mean by saying that both positions are relatively true is that if either position alone is carried to a logical conclusion, it ends either in absurdity or in a threat to the human condition.

50

The danger in absolutism, of course, lies in making false absolutes —that is, taking the credos and beliefs of a specific age and church and culture and converting them into immutable laws of God or nature. Theology became discredited in the past century largely because of this arrogant tendency. It is one thing to say that there are absolutes for man (which I happen to believe); it is quite another thing to say that we know utterly what such absolutes are, and that we speak with the voice of God. The dangers in moral absolutism, as in political absolutism, are tyranny, the repression of free inquiry, and the stifling of change.

The decline of the influence of the church — and indeed of all institutional authority in our century —has been in great part a reaction to absolutes that were seen to be false or at best half-truths. The rise of science, the spread of literacy, and the results of comparative anthropology have all combined to make modern man suspicious of any "law" that is universally embracing.

So many false and partial absolutes have been elevated and then abandoned that people become convinced that *all* absolutes are purely fictions created to maintain the authority of the status quo. Then the public, in the British phrase, "throws out the baby with the bathwater."

However, the dangers of moral relativism — for our time, at least — are as great, if not greater. Its chief threat lies in justifying almost anything, in making values a mere matter of taste or preference, in robbing us of all righteous indignation, and in replacing rational persuasion with brute force.

Most of all, as we are beginning to see today, moral relativism sets our children adrift and rudderless. Except for a vague sentimentality or humanitarianism that cannot weather the rough storms of mankind's irrationality and cruelty and duplicity, they are without a firm hierarchy of ethical values. (You may have noticed, incidentally, that the moral relativist almost always ends up as the tool of the powerful man who knows absolutely what he wants and absolutely how to get it.)

One of the reasons, I am convinced, that liberalism has been so weak a moderating force in modern European politics is that it has gone hand in hand with moral relativism, and the political absolutists of both left and right have overwhelmed liberalism by their sheer ruthless vitality. There is not any real "third force" between fascism and communism today because the liberal democrats don't really believe in a "right" or "wrong" that is based on any ethical imperative; as philosophical pragmatists, they have undercut their own humanistic roots.

"The best lack all conviction," said Yeats, "while the worst are full of passionate intensity." Many of the people we call good and decent and fair-minded are at the same time devoid of a firm hierarchy of ethical values. They may believe that some things are better than others, but they cannot defend their choices rationally; moreover, they are always tempted by expediency, by pragmatism, by the discredited maxim that "the ends justify the means."

This makes them immensely pliable at the hands of the false absolutists of our time — the communists, the fascists, the doctrinaires, the irrationalists of all sorts — who set up as absolutes such abstractions as the State, the Nation, the Proletariat, or the Party. Under these flags and for these dubious and transient loyalties, so-called decent people lie and conspire, traduce and kill — usually because they imagine they are opting for the "lesser evil." History tragically shows that when only two evils are offered as options, the lesser one usually turns out to be as disastrous as the greater if not more so.

At a deeper level of being, however, all people live by some hierarchy of values, private or public, admitted or tacit. The relativist may agree that whether one prefers chocolate or vanilla ice cream is purely a matter of sub-

The danger in
moral absolutism,
is of course
that of
tyranny and the
repression of free
inquiry and the
stifling of change.

jective taste; but when he is defending "the American way" or some other doctrine dear to his heart, you may be sure he believes it to be "better" — not just for him, but better in an absolute and objective sense. His relativism quickly disappears when his patriotism, his pride, or his pocketbook is touched. Otherwise, he would not argue his case; after all, how can a relativist hope to persuade someone whose self-interest may be different from his?

Let me try to explain, in nontechnical terms, what I mean by calling myself a "relative absolutist" and suggesting that there is a genuine polarity, and not a duality, between these two terms.

In the camp of the absolutists, classically speaking, we find the great tradition of Christian thought: Plato and Aristotle and St. Thomas Aquinas and so on down the line to such eminent neo-Thomists as Jacques Maritain and Etienne Gilson. These people, and all their hosts along with them, are variously known to philosophy as objectivists or realists or rationalists or humanists or any combination of these titles.

What they have in common is the conviction that man has been assigned a special nature by God (either Aristotle's prime mover or Thomas' personal deity, it matters not in this context) and that man's function is to fulfill his nature by obeying the laws of his being. These laws are eternal and immutable and may be known both by sacred scripture and by human reason. There is a direct line going from eternal law to natural law which commands us to behave in a way that is pleasing to God or consonant with Nature (Nature being conceived as a kind of Intelligence).

Interpreted correctly, and understood properly, this is a powerful and plausible argument, and not as easy to overthrow as some of its superficial opponents seem to believe. But, after believing it (at least in good part) for more than twenty years, I have come to the conclusion that it does not hold the philosophical water I would like it to hold. It is too narrow, too rigid, too formal, too concerned with essences and too little with existence, too preoccupied with specific acts, and too neglectful of ways of acting.

In the rival camp of relativists are ranged an equally impressive number of thinkers — starting with some of the pre-Socratic philosophers and going down to the modern scientists, behaviorists, logical positivists, linguistic philosophers, and naturalists of all shades and complexions.

What they have in common is the conviction that man is simply an object in the uni-

56

verse, a part of nature with a more highly developed brain, a molecular and chemical organism of nerves and blood and bone, differing only as a biological "species" from all other living creatures, and not endowed with any qualitative difference.

Being merely an animal, to these people, we ourselves have created our systems of morality just as we have created our artifacts. Religion, philosophy, ethics — these are purely man-made constructs and have no meaning beyond that which we care to give them. They are, in the broadest sense, conventions — ways of thinking, ways of controlling or expressing feelings, ways of organizing our personal and social lives — but they refer to nothing outside or beyond ourselves.

According to the naturalists, the behaviorists, and the positivists, what we call "mind" is simply a function of the brain; and everything speculative, mystical, or transcendental in our thought is little more than a figment of our imagination. As far as the extreme members of this group are concerned, if you can't see it, feel it, hear it, measure it, weigh it, or predict it, it might as well not exist — and for them, of course, it doesn't.

This, roughly, was my viewpoint for the twenty years preceding the other. I grew up as a typical product of late 19th century materialism, mechanism, positivism, Darwinism, and all the other "isms" that seemed so daring and free from conventional cant.

Eventually, I was forced to abandon this position. It contained too many self-contradictions; it ignored too many aspects of existence; it had its own dogmatic metaphysical presuppositions — the chief one being that it was anti-metaphysical.

Quite apart from the damaging practical consequences of relativism, the gravest charge against it is that if it is practiced as it is preached (and what good is a philosophy not acted upon?), it leads inevitably to nihilism — to an abandonment of all values — which would eventually mean the dissolution of society. For if "good" is only in the eye of the beholder, and if only "whether something works" determines its value, then whatever seems to work in the short run (however wicked or unjust) cannot be rationally opposed. The fact that it may not work in the long run is irrelevant to the relativist, for by the terms of his own belief, he has no business being concerned about what happens after he dies.

Between these two seemingly irreconcilable camps of Moral Absolutists and Moral Relativists there was until recently no philosophical position that could extract from each what was humanly useable, or could combine the sense in one with the sense in the other. They seemed to be contradictory positions, but it is my present belief that they are really contraries and that a genuine polarity may be established between them. This belief is held by a considerable number of modern philosophers who are attracted to that critical form of inquiry known as *phenomenalism*. This is not another "doctrine" or "school" of philosophy. Like existentialism, it is a way of *looking at* philosophical problems; it is an attitude and a mode of investigation. It is, in my view, the only mode of thinking that does full justice to the problems and paradoxes of 20th Century life.

CHAPTER FOUR

Morality and
The Authentic Person

Phenomenology is an attempt to seize the "fullness" of existence by combining what in the past have been seen as opposite tendencies, and therefore seems most admirably suited to handle a notion like polarity. It is a difficult concept to discuss on the popular level, but I shall do my best to explain its main principles.

Schools of philosophy in the past have been mainly "mentalist" or "materialist." One side concentrated on the mind and translated the universe into mental terms; the other concentrated on the physical universe and translated all mental activity into the motions of cells or atoms. (Naturally, there are subtle gradations and variations of this crude dichotomy I am making.)

The trouble with both these schools, according to the founder of phenomenalism, Edmund Husserl (who died in 1938), is that mentalists tend to swallow up the material universe, while the materialists tend to swallow up the mental universe. The phenomenologist is concerned with man-in-the-world, with the juxtaposition and relationship of the knower and the known *seen as an entity*. While the idealists slur the known in favor of the knower and the realists slur the knower in favor of the known, the phenomenologists try to deal with the entire gestalt as a unit, escaping between the horns of the mental-material dilemma. The world as seen through the personal and historical existence of man is the object of scrutiny; it is *relationship* rather than *essence* that provides the key to wider and deeper knowledge.

What does this imply in terms of morality? For the phenomenologist, there is a measure of truth in both the absolutist and the relativist positions. This measure has perhaps been best stated not by a philosopher, but by an economist, William A. Weisskopf.

In his book, *Alienation and Economics*, a brilliant analysis of moral relativism and the rise of the "economic man," Dr. Weisskopf makes this point about values:

> Ethics and morality are not merely epiphenomena and superstructures of the physical and of the actual, but the normative dimension is an essential characteristic of human existence. The creature called man knows that there are alternatives; he is confronted with the problem

of choice. Choice requires a standard for choosing, that is, moral and ethical norms.

The content of these norms is largely determined by society. However, it should be well understood that the normative is more than a social category. What we consider right and wrong may be influenced by social mores and attitudes; but the moral is a dimension of existence and not merely a social product. The normative dimension rests on consciousness, knowledge of alternatives, transcendence of the given situation and the necessity of choice —conditions which exist apart from society. This is not a metaphysical assumption but a phenomenological datum of human existence. Morality and the normative are rooted in the human predicament created by human knowledge of alternatives.

That is to say, the *content* of moral systems may change (though not as much as we think), but the moral imperative remains; value is part of man's beingness-in-the-world and not merely a social or cultural accretion; it is an essential part of the way we are made, like the shape of our teeth or the texture of our skin. To ignore the moral dimension or to regard it simply as a device that is used to mask self-interest or consolidate power is to violate an integral part of our basic makeup.

Then what does it mean, in actual practice, for me to call myself a "relative absolutist"?

What we consider
right or wrong maybe
influenced by social
mores and attitudes;
but the moral is a
dimension of existence
and not merely a social product

From a phenomenological point of view, it means that, in John Wild's words: "the moral ideal for man as such is to be authentically human."

Now I cannot *know*, through any books or rules or laws of logic, what it is to be "authentically human." I can learn it only by my own openness to experience.

Despite differences of culture, temperament, and upbringing, very different kinds of persons can be brought to agree on a general hierarchy of ethical values; indeed, all societies have had much the same values, however differently expressed. Truth, honesty, friendship, loyalty, fairness, kindness—these are preferred over lies, deceit, enmity, treason, partiality, and cruelty in virtually every society.

So far in human history, however, people have reserved these virtues for their "own" kind—first for the family, then for the clan and tribe, then for the city-state, the duchy, and finally the modern nation—which now commands the highest loyalty.

One way to become more "authentic"— becoming more what we were meant to be—is by expanding the exercise of these virtues to all of mankind, to the whole human race. Since the beginning of time, sages and saints and

65

prophets have pointed the way to this ultimate morality for man—but we have not yet reached that stage in our development where most of us are able or willing to treat everyone as a member of one family.

Since I believe, with Ortega, that man has no nature but only a history, I cannot be an absolutist in morals. Perhaps 4,000 years ago, birth control was "wrong" since it frustrated man's need to multiply and replenish the earth; today birth control may well be "right", if man's need as a species is to limit his population and thus avoid straining the ecological fabric beyond the breaking point.

On the other hand, I cannot be a relativist either, since I believe that there are normative truths that correspond to man's present needs and future development. These truths are not mere whimsies or preferences or social conventions but rather are emanations from his deepest (and still unknown) self.

For man is still more unknown to himself than anyone imagines—this is the building block of phenomenological study. We know more about the moon or the composition of a distant star than we do about ourselves, collectively or personally. Traditional philosophy investigated everything but the person who was doing the investigating, much in the posture of the familiar cartoon of the man searching desperately for his glasses while all the time they are out of sight perched on his forehead.

This is why Martin Buber has repeatedly stated that the most important discipline we must begin to delve into seriously is that of "philosophical anthropology"—not an anthropology that studies skulls or tribes or cultures, but one that studies man himself in the totality of his being. Then we can come nearer to answering the prime question "What is man?" This, as John Wild also stresses, is the key question of 20th Century ontological ethics. We have scarcely begun to frame the question, much less hope for a ready answer.

But the process of locating "man-in-the-world" is more a matter of collecting "non-answers" than of finding the "right" answer. It is a process of elimination in which we patiently pick up, scrutinize, and then discard pieces of the puzzle, laying them aside and saying, "No, this does not fit into the pattern." Hopefully, when we have collected enough non-answers (and in my view, every "ism" that now pretends to be a single answer is a non-answer), somewhere among what remains we shall be able to point to the target area, if not at the bull's-eye itself, which may be beyond human capability at present.

Before I leave the question of relativistic values, let me indicate how the relativization of values has permeated the whole fabric of modern society, not merely in morals, but also in cultural and intellectual areas.

The prevalent doctrine that "everything is a matter of taste or preference," that what may be good for one may not be good for another and that there is no way to arbitrate or judge these diverse tastes, has in my opinion debased and degraded the arts above all else. This relativization is in part responsible for the wretchedly low level of our public entertainment, in films, in music, in television, in the popular periodicals. "Giving the people what they want" is a false application of the democratic principle, for the arts are inherently aristocratic, not democratic—that is, they are designed to appeal to the *best*, not to the *most*. By the "best" I mean the most cultivated and the most competent to judge by reason of training and experience. (Let me hastily interject here that a true aristocracy tries to elevate everyone to a level of excellence and does not sneer superciliously at those who have not reached a ripe judgment.)

Consider the field of music. If you are an aesthetic relativist, one piece of music is as good as another, one composer is as talented as another. It all depends on what you happen to care for. If I like to hear Mantovani and you like to hear

Bach, I will call you a snob or a dictator for trying to tell me that my taste is worse than yours and that I should try to change my listening habits. Am I not entitled to like what I like?

Yes, but I am not entitled to proclaim that what I like is in any way equal to Bach. I am entitled to indulge in bad taste if I want to keep on diminishing myself, but I have no right to insist that what I get out of Mantovani is what you get out of Bach. I have the democratic right to be wrong in my aesthetic taste as much as in any other decision I make, but I have no right to be proud or smug in that choice; I must learn to recognize it as a deficiency in myself.

That there are definite levels in music can be demonstrated empirically. Almost all people, when they first begin listening to music, like those pieces that are obviously melodic and those with a pronounced beat and tempo. They find Bach or Mozart or Beethoven to be "difficult" or dull or unmelodic. If they keep up their musical education, and do not remain in the same rut, they gradually find that these simple and obvious pieces begin to bore them. Simple pieces exhaust their content in a few hearings. Because they are shallow and catchy, they have no lasting power and literally "play themselves out." Even a good second-rate composer like Ravel would drive us mad if we had to listen to his "Bolero" every day for a year.

The most significant thing about our "entertainment" today is that it does not entertain us very long.

Everybody who takes music seriously enough to learn more about it graduates in the same way from one level of composers to another. At first, if we go from popular music to serious music, we appreciate Grieg and Tschaikovsky and Rachmaninoff. They are sweet and melodic and romantic. But after awhile, we begin to yearn for something more substantial, more complex, more sophisticated in the true sense of that much-abused word. Then we go to Shubert and Brahms and up the ladder to Bach, Mozart, and Beethoven. Once we are there, we know we are home; we are where the core of music really resides.

The opposite never happens; it is a one-way street. No one has ever gone from an appreciation of Bach, Mozart, and Beethoven to an appreciation of Greig and Tschaikovsky. No composer, no performer, no genuine lover of music, and certainly no teacher, has ever appreciated the middle ranges as much as the heights after he has attained the heights. (The dying Tschaikovsky himself, in fact, expressed the adoring and envious wish that he could write one piece as well as Mozart.)

It is perfectly true that it is a matter of taste whether we prefer Bach or Mozart or Beethoven; here temperament plays a large part in which of these masters we would rather hear most of the time. At this peak of Parnassus, no one would dare judge the comparative merits of these geniuses. By the same token, it is much more than a mere matter of taste that they are inherently and objectively far superior to the Ravels and the Greigs.

Modern relativism in such matters has bred what I must call "the arrogance of ignorance." The average man no longer feels a demand or need to elevate his tastes, because "one man's opinion is as good as the next," even if one man enjoys Coca-Cola and the other savors the authentic essence of a vintage wine.

"Giving the public what it wants" rather than encouraging the development of taste is a self-defeating policy and ultimately an insult to the public itself. For the public does not know what it wants, except more of the same, and it quickly becomes tired of that. The incessant novelty, the quest for sensationalism, the whirligig of fads and fashions in popular art leave the public unsatisfied and constantly clamoring for the "new" because it has never learned to draw nourishing values out of the old.

The essence of a Shakespearean play or a Mozart quartet is that it contains infinite depths of meaning and pleasure; it is literally inexhaustible. A Shakespearean expert can read *Macbeth* fifty times and each time find some fresh insight in it. A music lover can listen to the last

Beethoven piano sonatas a hundred times, and each time hear some innuendo, some evocation, that he missed the last time.

Many people today simply refuse to believe this. They want to listen to only one kind of music, or read only one kind of book, under the delusion that they are "doing their own thing." But really doing your own thing, in the end, means doing what is most distinctively and permanently human, in all its dimensions; and nobody but the greatest artists has captured this full humanness in which each of us can share, individually and yet collectively. Relativism willfully closes its eye to the truth that great art is not an entertainment, but a summons to us to step across the threshold of humanhood.

CHAPTER FIVE

Polarities in Our Social and Political Institutions

In one of his most memorable passages, Lord Acton, that profound student of human affairs, remarked: "Every institution tends to perish by an excess of its basic principle." This statement grasps the whole idea of paradox and polarity in a dozen words. Acton meant that unless a system or institution includes at least a part of its complementary pole, not its opposite, it will die by applying its own single principle too rigorously and exclusively. Even a system as "open" and self-correcting as democracy is forced to draw the line somewhere. For as Bertrand Russell shrewdly observed, "A fanatical belief in democracy makes democratic institutions impossible."

Consider the two most crucial issues facing the United States in the 19th and 20th centuries. In the 19th century, the issue was domestic: slavery. In the 20th century, it was foreign: communism.

Despite differences of
culture, temperament
and upbringing,
very different kinds
of persons can be
brought to agree on a
general hierarcy of
etchical values;
indeed all societies
have had much the same
values, however differently
expressed. Truth, honesty,
friendship, loyalty, fairness,
kindness — these are preferred
in virtually every society over
lies, deceit, enmity, treason,
partiality, and cruelty.

Slavery in the South was doomed because it refused to moderate its basic principle that black men were not men, but merely property. When a system will give up nothing, it eventually loses everything. Likewise, czarism in Russia was doomed because it resisted any movement toward social democracy. Tyrannies break because they will not bend; and democracies crack and fall, as in the case of ancient Athens, because they do not maintain a proper tension between freedom and order.

Some historians of the Civil War period suggest that if the South had voluntarily freed its slaves, the white people there as much as the blacks would in the long run have benefited economically as well as socially and culturally. We would have avoided the dreadful wound of the Civil War (which is still festering), the reactive injustice of the Reconstruction period, and the eventual decline of the South as a productive region, when cotton lost its importance. Emancipation was not only morally right, but politically and economically sensible.

The South carried the principle of slavery to an excess hardly known anywhere else in the civilized world. (Slaves in other times and places could buy or earn their way to freedom.) This very rigidity destroyed the system and led the South into a century of decline, from which it is only now beginning to recover.

On the other side of the ledger, historians have suggested that the Union might have allowed the South to secede and become, in effect, another country. Eventually, the slave system would have collapsed of its own weight, and the prosperous free-labor industry of the North, compared with the dragging agrarian economy of the South, would have prompted the Confederates to sue for readmission to the Union on realistic and rational terms.

The intractability of both sides, leading inevitably to civil bloodshed and a hundred years of bitterness (culminating in the cancerous northern ghettos of today), sprang from their two-valued, black-and-white thinking, in which any compromise or equilibrium was ruled out by the passionate partisans in both camps. The cost America is paying for the Civil War—and the yet unresolved question of the black citizens' place in American society—is still mounting yearly and may finally even exceed our annual defense expenditures.

This takes us to our second issue—the Russian Revolution of 1917, the repercussions of which are still echoing around the world.

When the czarist government fell in Russia—and it fell as a rotten apple falls from a tree—the Western powers were so frightened of social democracy arising in Russia that they themselves actually helped to create the conditions of bolshevism—one of the great historical ironies of our time.

When the Kerensky government briefly took power in Russia—and it was a very mild, moderate, New Dealish kind of government—the Western Allies promptly stopped credits to Kerensky. As a result, his government fell, the Bolsheviks swept into power, and proved a thousand times more hostile to the Western nations than the moderates they succeeded.

Because the so-called democratic states were incapable of understanding the historical necessity for liberalizing the Russian system, they became in large part responsible for the subsequent successes of Lenin and Stalin and their followers.

(In much the same way, some forty years later, the United States propped up the corrupt and reactionary Batista regime in Cuba, which was so oppressive that it drove the people into the arms of left-wing revolutionaries. By the time we decided we had been wrong in supporting Batista and made belated efforts to aid the liberation movement, Castro had already captured the insurrectionist forces on behalf of communism.)

At the end of World War I, the rise of Hitlerism and the Nazi machine was facilitated by the deceitful and punitive attitude of the Allies, using the naive and idealistic President Woodrow Wilson as an unwitting cat's-paw. The nefarious Treaty of Versailles, the unrealistic reparations bill, and the subsequent economic crippling and moral dissolution of Germany provided a fertile soil for the cancer of Naziism to grow in. Indeed, it is hard to see what else could have grown in that poisoned atmosphere of Germany in the 1920s.

It is some small consolation, at least, that we seemed to have learned something of this bitter lesson after World War II—despite our asinine demand for unconditional surrender—when we rapidly proceeded to aid our former enemies, Germany, Italy, and Japan. We abandoned our duality of thinking—the good guys versus the bad guys—with generally gratifying results. The economy in these countries is healthy, and a basis was provided for a genuinely democratic structure.

After World War I, we *took*; after World War II, we *gave*. This was a tremendous step forward in comprehending the unitary nature of the post-atomic world and in forsaking the old dualistic ways of thinking.

But we have not yet learned enough. The major duality in our thinking today is that of something called communism versus something we like to speak of as the "free world." I think it is a false duality on several important counts.

In the first place, we are confusing economic systems and political systems. Communism, as practiced today, is two things: an economic system in which the state controls ownership, and a political system in which the state exercises supreme authority. However, these two are not *necessarily* connected. It is possible to have democratic socialism, as some of the Scandinavian countries do. In such cases, the people themselves freely decide how they want to run the economic system.

In the United States, and to a limited extent in some European countries, capitalism and democracy have traditionally gone hand in hand, but neither are these two *necessarily* connected. It is possible to have capitalism and a dictatorship, as in Spain. Indeed, several allies of the so-called free world are free in the economic sphere but repressive politically.

When we talk about being "against communism," it is important that we know what we are against. Public ownership, or state ownership, of the means of production may be foolish or unworkable or contrary to the best economic interest of a people; but there is nothing inherently immoral about it, so long as the citizens themselves freely choose it.

Tyrannies break because they will not bend; and democracies crack and fall, when they do, as in the case of ancient Athens, because they do not maintain a proper tension between freedom and order.

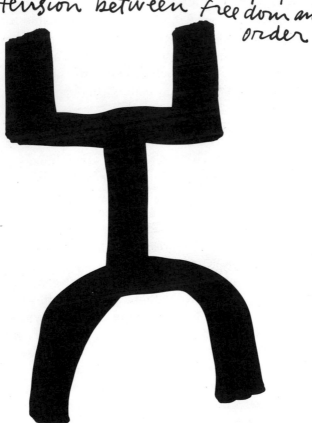

What is immoral about this system, as practiced in the Soviet Union and China and their satellites, is the political control exercised by a self-perpetuating elite over the masses of people. When the economic power and the political power are combined *in one group*, there exists a totalitarian society, which could be state capitalism or state socialism—it makes little difference what it is called.

What protects us in the capitalist countries is not capitalism, but our legal system and our tradition of civil liberties. The real division in the world today is not between ideologies, but between those nations that safeguard the basic rights of their citizens and those nations that violate such rights in the name of some "higher law." As Dr. Hannah Arendt puts it:

"The chief distinction today is not between socialist and capitalist countries but between countries that respect these rights, as for instance, Sweden on one side, the U.S. on the other, and those that do not, as, for instance, Franco's Spain on one side, Soviet Russia on the other."

It seems quite clear to me that the real argument between us and the Russians (or the Chinese) has little to do with communism and the free enterprise system. The Russians are not as doctrinaire as they were (because Marxist economics doesn't work as well as they had hoped it might), and we are not as "free enter-prisy" as we like to think and have not been for a long time (because classical capitalist econ-omics doesn't work as well as it did in the precorporate era).

At the risk of oversimplifiying, it might be said that the Russians are moving toward a form of state capitalism, and we are moving toward a form of private socialism—sometimes called Blue Cross!

Indeed, the American economy and social order over the past forty years is an interesting example of holding in tension—and in quite good tension, I think—the polarities of indi-vidualism and collectivism. As Frederick Lewis Allen remarked two decades ago, "America is not moving *toward* socialism—it is moving *beyond* socialism." What Allen means is that we are evolving a peculiarly "mixed economy." The American social and economic structure does not fit into any preconceived or doc-trinaire classification: it is a fluid combination of many trends and tendencies, some of them capitalistic and some of them collectivistic.

Marx and Engels predicted that capitalism would eventually fall of its own weight, because of its inescapable "internal contradictions." Their prophecy has so far proved false because, it would seem, capitalism has had enough resiliency, enough responsiveness, to adapt itself to changing conditions and indeed to learn something from the noncapitalistic orders.

We might even say—and rightly so—that the small, regular doses of socialism we have given ourselves have acted as an effective vaccine against the virus of communism.

(It is worth recalling that Marx predicted that communism would develop in "advanced" industrial countries, but, on the contrary, it has only arisen in "backward" agrarian countries, like Russia and China and Cuba, where the people lived under feudalism and had no experience living under democratic rule. The "advanced" countries anticipated the needs of the people and modified their practices to give the average person more security, more education, and more hope. Capitalism in the 20th century no more resembles what Karl Marx saw around him than communism today resembles what he envisioned for the future.)

If the Soviet Union stands against us today, it is not as a communist threat but as a very old-fashioned one—the threat of a powerful, repressive, ambitious nation-state, with a hunger for expansion and an intolerance towards any opposition, internal or external.

The polarity is not so much between two systems of thought or ideals or even economic practices as between two great powers who fear and suspect each other of hostile and aggressive intentions. This situation, of course, is older than the enmity between Athens and Sparta (which ultimately wrecked both city-states).

I suggest that this enmity cannot in any way be resolved or reduced by discussing it on the kindergarten level of communism. There is no rational reason why two competing economic systems cannot coexist in the world today—except that their political superstructures are in no way "rational."

What makes the coexistence difficult is not the differing ideologies, but the very structure of national power itself. There has never been room on this globe for more than one national power at a time.

Any resolution of this real opposition depends, it seems to me, not upon a victory for collectivism or for capitalism or any other "ism", but upon the creation and maintenance of a genuine world federalism, in which governments *can* compete economically without the power to compete militarily.

It seems axiomatic to me that we cannot have anything resembling world peace (we have only uneasy truces from time to time) until we have genuine world law; and we cannot have world law in any meaningful sense, until we persuade the nations to give up some of the "external" sovereignty they now cling to, more as a comforting fantasy than as a fact of life.

In the past, sovereignty had a substantial body of meaning. A city, a duchy, or a nation could defend its borders and could repel invaders. In the postatomic age, all that is possible is reprisal and retaliation. If Russia's atomic weaponry threatens to kill us ten times over, all we can do is threaten to kill them twenty times over. But once is all anyone can be killed.

There is also the technological fact that atomic war can be waged today without the victim knowing who the aggressor is. An atomic missile launched from a submarine can devastate New York or San Francisco. Who is the enemy? Before we know or can find out our hand is on the red button, and the world is plunged into irrevocable nuclear warfare. What measure of sovereignty exists under such conditions? Almost none.

Establishing world law and a world police to enforce it does not necessarily entail a monolithic superstate any more than the federal system in the United States entailed abolishing the several states. However, it does entail the willingness of the great powers to give up what they no longer freely possess anyway—the privilege of living in global anarchy.

The whole man
belongs to his tribe
and his group
and his nation,
but he must
also be, in some
way, above them;
he must see
himself
in the light
of eternity,
as a symbol
and
prototype
of what
mankind must become
in the future if it is
to survive and flourish.

The absence of a "fruitful tension" in society is most manifest where it is most needed: between national and international needs, in the area where our survival is most threatened. There is no real opposition between national identity and world welfare, rather there is a polarity between the two.

Given atomic weapons, it is obvious that no one single power can conquer the world, which will continue to have a number of power centers. The nation-state need not, and cannot, be "abolished"; it need only change its self-conception to accord with the realities of post-atomic warfare.

As Lady Barbara Ward Jackson has put it in her excellent book *Nationalism and Ideology*, the nation-state "will remain a lasting, constituent element in any worldwide supranational system, but it will not be the *ultimate* element. A 'unified' world should not mean a 'uniform' world where people are so many interchangeable parts; this would just be an Orwellian nightmare of 1984."

The issue today, Lady Jackson makes clear, is *function*, not *standardization*: "It is a sound principle of human order that social tasks should be left at the simplest and most human level at which they can be adequately performed—beginning with the family. Everyone understands the sense of a hierarchy of responsibility *inside* the nation. The central government does not overlay, just for the fun of it, the responsibility that can best be carried out by cities and counties or, in a federation, by the constituent states. But owing to the fixation of men's minds on *national* sovereignty, the top of the world's political pyramid is not there. We recognize authority and hierarchy up through all the levels of political, economic, and social need. Then, when at the highest level we reach the ultimate issues of survival itself, we recognize none. There is simply a blank arena, filled with the pressures and counter-pressures of irresponsible power. No one can call this reason. It represents a total failure of imagination and rationality."

This failure Lady Jackson so eloquently exposes is largely due to the false opposition we make between nationalism and supernationalism. These are false antitheses, because today each cannot survive without the other. There can be no sovereignty without security, and there is no security in our anarchic world.

Likewise, we must not frighten people with a view of a global government that will take over all functions and reduce the variety and diversity of peoples to a common mold. We must constantly stress the tension between the two, which can keep the nation-state flourishing and free from fear, while sustaining the world body in its peace-keeping functions. The old concept of warring dualism must be overcome by the new concept of sustaining polarity.

It seems to me that the real question today is not "Will we have a world government?" but "How will we get a world government and what will it be like?" There are only three possible answers to this: through conquest, through catastrophe, or through consent.

Establishing a world government might have been possible through conquest before the atomic age: a Caesar, a Napoleon, or even a Hitler might conceivably have unified the world under his terrible tyrannical heel. Now, retaliatory power is so immense that no single conqueror can ever again hope to establish such domination.

Catastrophe is another conceivable road to world government. If we do have an atomic war and if there are some survivors and if the earth is minimally habitable, then those few hundred or few thousand refugees from the debacle will of course have to form a world society simply in order to subsist. It will be too late then to be an Eskimo or a Frenchman or a First Family of Virginia. It will be the *last* families who unite, but at what painful cost this lesson of common humanity will have been learned.

The third possible answer is by consent — by enough people realizing the futility of any other answer and deciding to give up a part of their national pride and false sense of independence in order to assure the continuation of our species on earth. Only our youth, so far, seem to be clear-sighted enough to understand this; and youth all over the world are joining hands to proclaim a unity that has often been preached but never before seriously practiced.

There is, of course, one factor weighing heavily in our favor today — the unfeasibility of modern war. President Kennedy admitted it; Mr. Khrushchev admitted it. War as an instrument of national policy has become obsolete because it can no longer be controlled. This is not to say that war may not happen; it is all too likely to happen by accident, escalation, a fit of insanity, or any number of incalculable factors. In their more sober moments — when they are not boasting and brandishing the latest weapons of overkill — world leaders agree that nobody could win the next war, that everybody would lose.

The enormous and fantastic fallacy that we can any longer have winners and losers in a war is the final duality that must topple in the modern world.

This has always been a false duality, because the end of one war always bred the germs of the next. But mankind clung to the illusion that there were victors and vanquished. Now science—by accelerating the process of destruction so rapidly—has begun to tear this illusion from our eyes.

Our potential for destruction, has now, in the words of one expert, "become so promiscuous, so irreversible, and so incalculable" that every thinking person on both sides of all curtains knows in his heart that the next war will mean total annihilation, not just for us, but for "the very seed and protoplasm of the human species." The next war will not merely kill men, women, and children in far greater numbers; it will "distort the very *nature of man* within the structure of the germ-cell itself."

What L. L. White calls "the unitary man" must prevail over the dualistic man. We can no longer afford to think in terms of Us and Them; we must learn to think (and to feel), in Buber's terms, of I-and-Thou. When we can do this, if we ever can, then we will have begun to approach our true humanhood; we will begin to know that an essential part of I is in Thou and an essential part of Thou is in I.

CHAPTER SIX

The Obsolescence of Dualism In a Converging World Community

No principle, no concept, no idea, and no system is valuable or long viable unless it learns to tolerate, to absorb, and to maintain an equilibrium with the Other. Not with its "opposite" —truth cannot temporize with falsehood—but with its Yin and its Yang sustaining and complementing each other. The sweetness needs the salt for taste; the light needs the darkness for contrast; the individual needs the society; the pursuit of competition requires the restraint of cooperation; the masculine personality in men must be tempered by some feminine traits, just as the feminine personality must be endowed with some masculine traits, or both become monsters and not human beings.

But this is not saying that everything can, or must, be resolved in a dialectic. The Germanic philosophers, with their passion for "system-building," invented a theory of dialectic wherein the polar opposites merged or blended into a higher "synthesis." This was carried to its height by Hegel, and then turned upside down by Marx in his dialectical materialism.

Simply put, Hegel believed that any thesis of thought must meet its antithesis of thought, and the result is a synthesis at a higher level. Marx borrowed this concept and applied it to history, where he saw the opposition between the working classes (thesis) and the bourgeoisie (antithesis) culminating in the synthesis of a classless society.

The idea of polarity is not compatible with that of dialectic. In the first place, dialectic is an intellectual construct that is often forced or contrived, and not found in nature. There is no reason to believe that oppositions will ever unite into a higher type exhibiting a new form. Men and women will not turn into a unisex; the economic conflict between the working classes and the middle classes may as easily result in fascism as in communism; and there is nothing deterministic in nature or human conduct that guarantees an ultimate unity of opposites.

It is important to understand this difference; otherwise we run the risk of becoming doctrinaire and dogmatic in our views. There is nothing "inevitable" in human affairs; events do not follow any "laws of thought."

As an illustration of dogmatic thinking, let us take a look at the two sorts of extremists in our country today on the subject of war and peace. Both sorts are equally dangerous, in diametrically opposed ways.

On the one hand, we have the extremists who insist that war is inevitable. The world has always had and will always have wars, and there is simply no answer to the problem. The most we can do is to arm ourselves as heavily as possible, prepare to go underground when the time comes, and enjoy ourselves in the interim as much as possible.

The other extreme is more sophisticated, but equally fallacious. These people insist that war is now out of the question. The very magnitude of atomic conflict, the very horror of it, the very finality of it—all these stand as guarantees that it cannot and will not happen. For each side in the conflict knows that the other has the power to annihilate it completely. Through mutual fear of destruction—balance of terror, it is called—the great behemoths will refrain from using their nuclear weaponry.

In my considered opinion, both these extremist positions are perilously, tragically, and fatally wrong. While they are diametrically opposed in their analysis of the future, they lead to quite similar attitudes: inertia, resignation, the rigidity of defensiveness, or the passivity of heedless optimism.

The polaristic position says that war is neither inevitable nor inconceivable, but *possible*. It says that alternatives are open to us,

97

if we but explore them, that we are not the blind pawns of fate or circumstance or science or the bestiality of human nature, and that we can learn to change and modify the mood and direction of our thinking and our energies. It says that war will most likely come if we do nothing or if we do the wrong things. War can be avoided if we decide—earnestly and deeply—to surpass the Russians, not in weapons and strategies and the capacity for overkill, but in imagination, ingenuity, moral courage, wisdom, and the resourcefulness we have shown in so many other less important areas.

I think the great majority of the American people would agree with this position, with this attitude, for it is a position both radical and conservative in the best sense of both these ancient and honorable words. It is *radical* in the original meaning of the word, for it wants to go to the *roots* of the problem, and that is what radical originally meant. It is *conservative* in the classical sense of that word because it wants to conserve the civilization it has taken us so many thousands of years to build; it wants to conserve the values that alone make life meaningful.

Yet, despite the eminent rightness of this position, it must be admitted that the American public has remained generally passive toward nuclear policy. Why should this be so when their very lives and their children's lives are at stake?

There are a number of marginal reasons. For one, until quite recently, the word *peace* was a dirty word in America, that was somehow associated with subversive or suspicious groups who manipulated this word for their own ideological purposes. Then, again, we are notoriously a people who worship size and strength for their own sake, and any group suggesting that size and strength cannot save us from global catastrophe is thought to be unduly pessimistic and negativistic.

But the real reason for our passivity, I believe, lies in our unconscious belief in magic. The great mass of people, who don't agree with the extremists that war is either inevitable or inconceivable, *do* believe, in some unconscious and tenacious way, that problems will solve themselves if we ignore them and pretend they are not there. This is our great human capacity for willful self-delusion. It has been responsible for ninety percent of the world's woes from the beginning of time.

We can see this self-delusion operating in every area of social activity. For a hundred years we hoped that the "Negro problem" (which is really a "white problem", of course) would go away if we ignored it; we hoped that by some

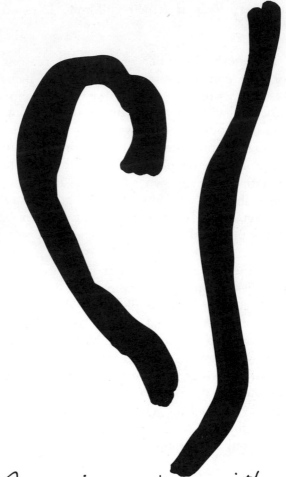

There is no love without a
tinge of hate, and no hate
. without at least a
        trace of attraction.

magic the blacks might turn white or disappear or actually come to enjoy the way they were treated. By the time we got around to looking at the problem seriously—and then only because we were forced to—it was nearly out of hand.

So what do we have to do to keep face with ourselves psychologically? We have to accuse the blacks of "wanting to go too far too fast" —after a century of *Caucasian* inertia, mind you!

We still believe that some sort of magic will save our cities, which are gradually being eroded by slums and cheap commercial exploitation and venal politics—at least some still believe it. Those who believe in a different magic have moved to the suburbs, where the same problems will pursue them a decade later.

Juvenile deliquency, mental illness, housing problems, prison reform, pollution, education— one cannot name a major area of social activity that has not been the victim of this belief in magic, this grotesquely irrational conviction that somehow things would straighten themselves out if we only gave a few dollars to the Crusade for Mercy and got rid of our crabgrass.

So it is hardly surprising, therefore, that when a problem so overwhelming, so pulverizing, so demanding of concern and dedication and complete humanhood as "total war" arises, that we should invoke this belief in magic to the ultimate degree. For war is the ultimate and most existential question that has ever faced the human race.

We know what most of our congressmen and political leaders are like. We know what the military mind through the ages has been like. We know what meagre information we possess about the actualities in our own country, much less elsewhere in the world. Yet, knowing all this, we cling to the superstition that the gods will favor us, that we are too young and good to die, that the ugly frog will turn into a prince and save us from the dragon.

What we need to be saved from is ourselves —from our naivete, our relentless optimism, our resolute sentimentality, our monumental indifference, and our profound moral inertia.

We as a people must refuse to abdicate our personal responsibilities as citizens and rational creatures endowed with intelligence and free will. We must give up, difficult though it may be, our primitive belief in magic in this most mechanized and scientific of ages. We must make an effort to get the facts, to understand the issues, to comprehend the decisions before us—because making no decision or letting others make it for us is the surest way to dissolve the democratic process.

This is the profound and chilling paradox of contemporary society: we may be told we are fighting for our lives, but we have lost the capacity to make a rational decision based on known facts.

In the greatest age of science, we are thrown back utterly on faith—on faith in a handful of men no less fallible than we. These men are entrusted with power a trillion times greater than the world has ever known before. What security do we have against their errors, their miscalculations, their pride and prejudice and plain mortality?

Yet, the inestimable advantages of a democratic society are that issues *can* be forced into the open, public men *can* be called to account, and public opinion *can* defeat private machinations. This is both the weakness and the towering strength of democracy. It gives us less cohesion than the dictatorships and much more flexibility, which has always been the key to survival. (The dinosaurs died out because they could not adjust to their changed environment.)

Nations that cannot change always perish; they become obsolete and easy prey to internal dissolution or foreign attack. We must learn to change faster than ever before in history—to change our ways of thinking and our perspec-

But really doing your own thing,
in the end, means doing what
is most distinctively and permanently
human, in all its dimensions;
and nobody but the greatest
of artists has captured this
full humanness in which each
of us can share,
individually and yet collectively.

tives, to change our hierarchies of private and public values, and most of all, to change our *national self-conception.*

We must learn to wish for and to work for what is good for mankind as a whole. There is no individual salvation without world salvation, and there is no world salvation without individual effort, small and inconsequential though it may seem. The question we often ask ourselves is "What can one person do?" One person can do little, but one and one and one and one can do a great deal.

In World War I, Clemenceau said: "War is too important to be left to the generals." More than fifty years later, we must say that science has become too dangerous to be left to the scientists, and politics too fatal to be left to the politicians.

CHAPTER SEVEN

The Personal Paradox:
The Individual and the Collective

Proust, in his great novel, *Remembrance of Things Past*, remarks: "The universe is the same for all of us, and different for each of us." This is the deepest metaphysical paradox that we need to grasp and cling to at all times.

The universe is the same for all of us—we have the same needs, the same loves, the same fears, the same rights, the same obligations. And the man who denies this in the name of "individualism" becomes a spiritual fascist, a dehumanized creature, an exploiter and oppressor.

The universe is different for each of us—for each of us is a distinct, unique human personality, with his own contribution to offer, his own independence and autonomy, his own freedom to make decisions. And the man who denies this in the name of "society" or "historical forces" becomes an authoritarian collectivist, and cruelly sacrifices living personal values for an abstract future that can never be realized under his totalitarian concept of mankind.

Between the extreme of the "individualist" on the one hand, and the "collectivist" on the other, we need to hold to the idea of the "person"—who is both more than an individual and more than a part of a collectivity, but shares in both, at different times and in differing ways.

As Martin Buber has so forcefully pointed out, individualism is too narrow a philosophy, and collectivism too broad, for the human spirit. We speak of individualism and collectivism as if they were contradictories, and as if we had always to choose between the one and the other. What we fail to see is that each of them is equally bad without its complementing polarity. As Buber puts it: "Individualism understands only a part of man; collectivism understands man only as a part. Neither advances to the wholeness of man, to the human person as a unity."

Individualism and collectivism are not contradictories, but contraries that can be reconciled only by recognizing that personalism, or the "human person," is the ultimate source of meaning and value in the universe.

Fragmented from its polarity, the sin of individualism leads to self-centeredness—to indifference about others except as they serve our own ends. And, equally, fragmented from its polarity, the sin of collectivism is the idolatry of turning Society into a god, and stifling personal values for an illusory future social goal. Only by using the human person as a touchstone of our thinking and feeling can we avoid these twin errors of reaction or repression.

(The semantic reason, incidentally, that "individualism" has become such a respected word in the American lexicon is its early historical association with independence and the freedom from social or political restraints that characterized the American Revolution; actually, we have turned into an exceedingly conformist people, deeply suspicious of individualism in thought, action, or dress, and honoring the notion only in the field of economic competition.)

Subsuming the polarities of individualism and collectivism under the rubric of Personalism, it becomes evident that turning oneself into a "fuller person" is the ultimate task of each of us, just as the aspiration of the acorn is to become the "most" oak tree it can be. Our final goal, then, is not success or prestige or dominance or the satiation of appetites, but *becoming what we are meant to be*. This, of course, is the core meaning of "authenticity."

To become a fuller person, in any meaningful and productive sense of the term, one must

... it is the feeling of emotional security that gives us genuine freedom, and it is the freedom to express our inner selves that gives us an abiding sense of security.

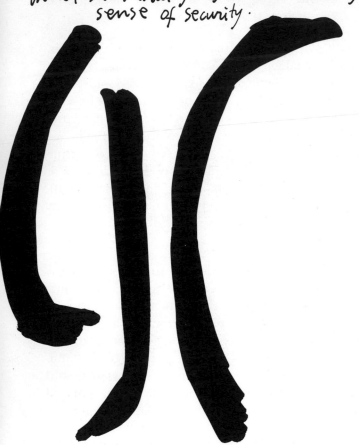

begin by recognizing two things at once—in themselves a seeming paradox: first, that the good of the community is more important than the good of any one individual; and, second, that the good of the community consists in bringing the good life to all the persons who comprise it. If we ignore, or neglect, either of these polarities in our public life, we risk the peril of falling into the grand errors of Marxism or reaction.

Some of the dilemmas (in paradoxical form) abounding in our affluent society can be resolved or reduced only by concentrating on the Personalist approach to the problems of the commonwealth. For instance:

——As we get richer, we get poorer.

——As we get stronger, we get weaker.

——As we get larger, we get smaller.

What do these apparently contradictory statements mean?

"As we get richer, we get poorer," means that we have begun to learn, in the last decade, that the rich society is impoverishing its environment and its non-renewable resources at an alarming rate. The more we produce and consume, the faster we use up our resources and strain our facilities. As we increase our Gross National Product, we shorten the time left in which to restore a balanced ecology to the earth, or an equitable balance between the haves and the have-nots.

"As we get stronger, we get weaker," means that a nation with tremendous atomic power, such as ours, is severely limited in its options. We must tread carefully lest we provoke an atomic holocaust. Meanwhile, our possession of atomic weapons inspires other nations to build them, so that our relative position is weaker than in pre-atomic times, when a large army and conventional weapon superiority were possible deterrents against aggression.

(Also, as more and more countries acquire atomic capability, our numerical superiority becomes meaningless, especially since these smaller countries have "less to lose" in an all-out atomic war.)

"As we get larger, we get smaller," means that as our population increases, and our technology becomes more complex, the individual shrinks in importance. Even the power of towns, cities and states becomes insignificant in terms of such problems as pollution, race relations, education, transportation, and others. Yet, at the same time, there is a greater need for individual participation

112

in the decision-making process; otherwise we become swallowed up in a gigantic bureaucracy so busy with administrative procedures that it forgets the human ends for which these policies were originally devised.

Such modern paradoxes, and others like them, account for the vast ambivalences in today's value-system at all levels—in our attitudes toward science, toward religion, and toward government.

In the area of science and technology, we appreciate and eagerly utilize the benefits they have conferred upon us; on the other hand, we fear that large impersonal mechanisms are reducing the importance of the individual, making us cogs in a vast machine, the purposes and ends of which we can only anxiously guess at.

Our contemporary religious attitude is another example of ambivalence. On the one hand, most persons believe in the importance of faith and the necessity for some sort of continuing tradition; on the other hand, many persons, especially youth, have found institutional religion increasingly irrelevant to the basic concerns of society, for its failure to confront boldly the social, economic and racial tensions in our country and throughout the world.

Individualism is too narrow a philosophy, and collectivism too broad, for the human spirit. These contraries can be reconciled only by recognizing the "human person" as the ultimate source of meaning and value in the universe.

Our attitude toward government is even more frustratingly ambivalent. On the one hand, we expect government to protect and preserve what we have—an attitude implicit in the loud demand for "law and order," which is largely a call for maintaining the status quo at all costs. On the other hand, we resist and resent what we term "government interference" in areas that might adversely affect our social or economic self-interest.

We are for a "free market" when government controls threaten our autonomy, but then remain strangely acquiescent toward such flagrant manipulations of the free market as subsidies, cost-plus contracts, monopolies and oligopolies, price-fixing, import duties and oil-depletion allowances.

Our so-called "public philosophy" is an *ad hoc* patchwork of inconsistencies and contradictions, without any firm framework of meaning or coherence. We are for "stronger laws" when hoodlums or unions threaten our persons, our properties, or our profits, but for "weaker laws" or "fewer laws" when it is proposed that some of our advantages be curtailed or our privileges revoked.

Many Americans, for instance, want our government to be as strong and dominant as possible in foreign affairs, but weak in domestic affairs, which is an impossible contradiction. A government that spends more than half its annual budget on defense is, in effect, controlling the economy. Such control must inevitably be reflected in domestic affairs.

If we begin to understand the legitimate and fulfilling needs of the human person—and are not beguiled by the false gods of either individualism or collectivism— then our ambivalences about science, about religion, and about government, fall into their proper perspective in modern society.

We can then examine, and at least partly resolve, these ambivalences by starting with the framework of paradox, using the notion of polarity, and applying the principle that the person is the unit of concern—and thus beginning to work our way out of this intellectual and emotional confusion.

As an obvious example of the reordering of priorities, science must become the servant of man, and not its master, as it threatens to be. It should not be used, as we do in the United States, to amass huge profits for a few entrepreneurs, or, as in the Communist countries, to further the aims of an ambitious bureaucratic elite. The spending of $20 billion—one-fifth of our national budget—for a project to send an American to the moon (largely for reasons of national prestige) was criminally wasteful while we continue to tolerate slums and inferior schools and proliferating crime and pollution and family alienation.

Science itself is obviously a neutral medium; atomic fission can be used to make bombs or to create tremendous energy that would relieve much of the world's crushing poverty. Both our individualism and the Russians' collectivism lead toward the former; a mature personalism would lead to the latter.

In the area of religion, which is composed of two primary elements—love of God and love of fellow man—we find that these components have become severed in the modern world. In any true and workable religious synthesis, the demands of piety and the requirements of social justice must be held in equilibrium. Unfortunately, today many "religious" people are unconcerned about social justice, while the activists in the social area are often lacking in the love and compassion that alone can restrain their movement from degenerating into mob-rule and eventual despotism in the name of "equality."

In his admirably concise overview of our contemporary problems, *Tangled World*, Roger Shinn of Union Theological Seminary has warned that religion must face up squarely to the question of basic involvement in problems of living: "It must not offer merely consolations, rituals, or the frigidity of theological conformity." Religion needs a bold and existential approach to the questions that confront and baffle modern man: the questions of personal identity and social relations, war and peace, wealth and poverty, security and freedom, happiness and unhappiness.

In the realm of government and public policy, the welfare of the person must be our guiding criterion. Fulminating against the "welfare state" is both cruel and thoughtless, for we must recognize that people have no true freedom until they have a minimal measure of security. Freedom is a social relation, not an act of the will—contrary to what most people imagine, Robinson Crusoe, living alone on his island, had no freedom whatsoever; he was simply a child of nature, like any other animal. Freedom begins only when restraints between people are mutually self-imposed and self-regulated.

The ancient opposition of conservatism and liberalism, as we have traditionally understood them, are obsolete in the technocratic and corporate state of our time. Conservatives can no longer place profits above people; liberals can no longer place programs above people; both profits and programs must be subordinated to human ends, rather than to some rigid ideology.

118

The ideal to reach for may be the one suggested by Dorothy Thompson many decades ago, in her prescription to be "a radical as a thinker, a conservative as to program, and a liberal as to temper." While this eclectic goal may never be achieved, it points the way to a creative tension between contraries directed toward the common purpose of serving the person instead of subjugating him to any "ism."

CHAPTER EIGHT

Modern Man:
Paradox in Process

Because of our distinctively new self-image in this latter part of the 20th Century, and because the external conditions of life have been changing at an exponential rate, we have been forced to question our value-system in every area, from religion to education to sexual relations.

Many of our ancient values are toppling, and some are disappearing altogether. Some of them deserved to disappear, being the fossilized inheritance of ages that faced very different problems. Others need to be retained. It is hard to separate the one from the other, but that is our task. It is this that makes us so uneasy and anxious. How can we distinguish between "eternal truths"—if there are any—for man, and those maxims that have outlived their usefulness and must be revised or rescinded?

You cannot find the answer in any book. There is no single teacher or preacher who can provide a simple, unified solution or prescrip-

We can no longer,
like Voltaire's Candide,
go home and quietly
cultivate our own
gardens -- for nothing
will grow in gardens
tomorrow, on the
day after, on the year
after, unless we are
willing to help
transform god's
earth into a garden
for all
families
every-
where,
who ask only for the
same privilege.

tion for our ills. What confronts us is an existential problem that each man and woman must face in spiritual nakedness.

There are, however, some new tools at our disposal. We can learn a lot from scientific methodology—that scrupulous discipline which forces us to examine and reexamine our preconceptions and to test them against empirical reality.

We can learn something from depth-psychology, and the magnificent contributions of Freud and his colleagues can help us enormously—if, again, we know what to accept and what to reject in that canon of belief. For Freudianism can become a religion for many, just as Marxism has; and no single discipline is big enough to encompass the fullness of man's religious needs.

Most of all, we must, with all our might, resist the tendency—so strong in our industrial society—to become "functions" of men, rather than whole men. We must learn to be "self-centered" in the original sense of that word; that is, our central concern must be with ourselves as men, in the fully human aspects of our being. As Paul Tillich has pointed out, industrial man is only a part of man; psychological man is only a part of man; even religious man is only a part of man: "The isolation and imperialism of any one aspect of the personality is one of the greatest threats facing us today." The result of this is likely to be depersonalization and dehumanization, which too often may end in a smug and morally imbecilic Eichmann "doing his duty."

Our great need is to learn to see ourselves as "the whole man" (and the whole woman, too, of course), not just as the consumer, the businessman, the taxpayer, the suburbanite, or even the American. Each of us is greater, more complex, and more worthwhile than any society to which we belong—and yet, as the ultimate paradox, unless we place the needs of that society before our own, both we and it will perish in our own suicidal short-sightedness.

Without this vision, and this determination to become more than a mere "function" of a person, humanity faces the twin bleak prospects of degenerating into greedy and heedless individualism, or into the collective drabness and despotism of an anthill society. The only way to prevent either of these disasters is to cling to the concept of the *person* and to recognize that all other values must be placed at the service of our personhood; that is, fulfilling all the potentials of what we were meant to be, individually and as a species.

To become, in Abraham Maslow's term, a "self-actualizing person" is a difficult job, but without it, no other job has much meaning, or, in the end, much joy.

As the first step in developing our person-hood, we must learn from the three basic revolutions of the last century that many of the old "opposites" do not exist, and never did. We have already learned that time and space are aspects of the same continuum; that body and mind are unitary and not just complementary; that matter and energy are convertible into one another. Thus, many ideas formerly thought to be "dualities" are now seen as polarities that need, balance or sustain each other. We must now begin to apply this lesson to our social structure, to our political entities, to our personal relationships.

If we can hold the polarities of individualism and collectivism in good tension when considering social or political or economic measures, we will then not ask ourselves such outmoded and unproductive questions as, "Does it promote individualism?" or "Will it lead to socialism?" but a much more basic question "What does it mean in terms of the human spirit and personality?"

Some forms of individualism are wholesome and necessary, while other forms are merely licenses to violate the common good; some collective measures are needed to protect the

It is not so much
the kind of disease
a person gets as
the kind of person
who gets the disease...

human person from want and injustice, and some collective measures pose a threat to the human person. It is our task to make such distinctions, not blindly to support or oppose any given measure on the basis of some preconceived ideology that is irrelevant to the human condition here and now.

Perhaps the most dangerously false duality in the public mind is that existing between the so-called "spiritual" and the "material." Many people, in reflecting on our modern dilemmas, say to themselves and to others: "What we need is an increase in spirituality. Material things have become too important. We need a return to spiritual values, and then we would be able to live together in peace and harmony."

But, as Reinhold Niebuhr has sharply reminded us: "Too often we ask that religion not only ease our fears, but that it relieve us of social responsibility." We use spirituality as an escape from reality, link it with God, and leave it at that. It then serves as "an escape from moral decisions in the social realm."

Many, if not most, people who consider themselves Christians look upon the spiritual as the "opposite" of the material, when in truth they are inseparable polarities. There is no break between the two; both must be held in a creative tension at the same time. This is why, in the Old Testaments, the priests enjoined piety, and the prophets railed against social injustice; and, in the New Testament, Jesus identified himself with the poor, the afflicted, the outcasts, the exploited, as much as he preached the Second Coming.

Man is uniquely a creature who *cannot* realize his spiritual nature unless and until he translates it into his social nature. There is no way to be genuinely spiritual except through one's intentions and acts toward others; no way to "love God" (except as mere sentimentality), without loving each of His children.

(This is why, as many modern theologians have stressed, in the Judaic and Christian faiths, the love of God and the love of fellow man are *equated*. The double commandment of Jesus, "Thou shalt love the Lord thy God," and "Thou shalt love thy neighbor as thyself," indicates that the spiritual life cannot be healthy if the social life is built on superiority, selfishness, or callous indifference.)

Modern man has scarcely begun to unite these principles. We have not fused the spiritual and the social; instead we hold our beliefs, as it were, in air-tight compartments. "Religion" is something we take part in on Sunday, like bowling on Tuesday; it permeates little, if at all, into our business, professional, social or civic activities.

Some twenty years ago, Albert Cardinal Meyer, then Archbishop of Chicago, reminded his flock of something that clergymen of all faiths should remind theirs:

"It is a mystery why some Catholics think that men go to hell only for sins of impurity, for missing Holy Mass, or for eating meat on Friday. They do not remember that defrauding the poor man of his wages is a sin that cries out to heaven, or that dishonesty in business or professional life, or the corrupt exploitation of public office, are even more serious than private sin, because they directly injure the common good of all. Unless a Catholic fulfills his duties to society . . . he endangers his soul."

A large share of the current youth rebellion —not only in the United States, but throughout the world—is directed against the artificial opposition we have set up between our Christian preachments and our un-Christian practices; against our narrow definition of "sin" as a personal or private transgression, and our refusal to acknowledge that our neglect of the poor, our treatment of the blacks, our preoccupation with gain and our support of aggressiveness, are darker sins than we dare to admit.

Most of us today are intensely concerned with the private, the personal, the intimate, and the familiar; but unless we can hold these con-

The question we often
ask ourselves is
"What can one person
do?" One person can
do little — but one
and one and one
and one can do a
great deal.

cerns in a fruitful tension with the social, the political, the racial, and the international, we are erecting impenetrable iron curtains in our own minds and hearts.

It is no longer possible, as it was for Voltaire's Candide, to go home and quietly cultivate our own gardens. For, as the ecologists and the atomic physicists increasingly remind us, nothing will grow in gardens tomorrow, or the day after, or the year after, unless we are willing to help transform God's earth into a garden for all families everywhere, who ask only for the same human privilege.

Explanation of Terms

ABSOLUTISM
Another term for "Objectivism," the doctrine that certain moral principles can be known by reason, faith, or intuition, and that such principles are universally and eternally binding upon man.

ABSTRACTION
A process of separating the inherent qualities or properties of something from the actual physical object to which it belongs; the formation of a concept, directing attention to its generalized nature rather than to any specific example.

ALIENATION
A term used by existentialists to refer to the estrangement of the self from itself or from others; also used earlier by Marx to refer to the industrial workers' loss of identity in mass society.

AUTHENTIC EXISTENCE
A way of responding, by choice or decision, to the condition of one's humanhood, such as the mode of relating to others, facing death, or exercising conscience at a level beyond that of the conventional.

AXIOLOGY
A branch of philosophy that considers the existence, nature, and criteria of value and disvalue.

BEHAVIORISM
A psychological school based soley on physiological and neurological observed data, refusing to take into account such unobservable phenomena as mind or consciousness. Closely allied to Positivism. (q.v.)

CONCEPT
A thought or concentrated awareness, as distinct from percept or image, usually projected by abstraction and derived from specific instances or events.

DETERMINISM
A philosophical (and sometimes psychological) doctrine that all events are governed by causes outside, or preceding, themselves.

DIALECTICS
In Plato, a form of inquiry by questions and answers which reveal and test implicit assumptions; in Hegel, "dialectical" logic consists of a thesis, its antithesis, and their final resolution into synthesis. Later, Marx applied this Hegelian form of reasoning to his materialist interpretation of history.

DUALISM
A view that the world, or any aspect of it, is divided twofold between related but separate or antagonistic elements: such as the Mind-Body duality in psychology, the Good-Evil duality in theology, or the Mind-Matter duality in metaphysics.

EMPIRICISM
The view that all human knowledge is derived from experience, by means of sensation, with or without some sort of immediate awareness of mental acts. Is usually contrasted with Rationalism. (q.v.)

ESSENCE
The nature of *whatness* of anything, by virtue of which it is what it is, or what defines it as belonging to a particular class.

ETHICS
A branch of philosophy dealing with the meaning and application of "good" and "right" for man in his relations with others; also, the study of the ultimate human ends, both individually and socially.

EXISTENTIAL
An adjective loosely characterizing all those philosophers and thinkers who agree—despite their differences—that the concrete, individual, human existence is the

134

proper starting-point for all speculation, rather than the general and universal axioms of classical philosophy.

MANICHAEISM
A form of religious thought imported to the early Christian world from India, in which cosmic history is depicted as a conflict between the forces of light (representing the Spirit) and the forces of darkness (representing Matter). This primitive dualism was declared heretical by the early church largely because of its denial of the goodness of Creation.

MATERIALISM
A metaphysical theory that is anti-metaphysical insofar as it asserts that all reality is simply matter in motion, with everything that appears to be "mental" or "spiritual" being in actuality a manifestation of matter.

NATURALISM
A philosophical doctrine that nothing exists outside the world of nature, and that what is called "supernaturalism" is either a delusion or a mode of nature not yet apprehended by man. While all materialists are naturalists, not all naturalists are materialists.

NATURAL LAW
In Aristotle, and especially in Aquinas, the theory underlying moral philosophy, viz., that human reason can discern what is "right" or "good" for us, and that every human act can be determined to be either in accord, or in violation of, the natural law by the proper exercise of reason.

PARADOX
From the Greek, meaning "what is against common opinion"; has come to mean any statement that seems to be self-contradictory or which is true and false at the same time; it was brought forth as a philosophical tool by Kierkegaard, who felt that ordinary reason could not penetrate to the ultimate categories of existence.

PERSONALISM

The view, held by a diversity of thinkers, that human personality is the touchstone of all philosophy, and that ultimate value is grounded in the human person as the highest form of reality. Like the existentialists (whom they resemble to some degree) personalists may be either theistic or atheistic.

PHENOMENOLOGY

Technically, the study of appearances in human experience, which tries to apprehend the universal "structure" in the phenomena of that experience, while leaving out of account all considerations of objective reality and the purely subjective response of the investigator.

POLARITY

A relation between seeming opposites, each of which is independent but finds its completion in cooperating with its polar opposite, by intensifying, limiting, qualifying, or supporting the other in synergistic fashion.

POSITIVISM

A movement founded in the 19th century by Auguste Comte, which has now come to mean any speculation that severely limits itself to matters of fact and sense experience, and denies validity to any observations not derived from fact, logic, or mathematics.

PRAGMATISM

The doctrine that the "truth" or "value" of an idea rests in its practical consequences rather than in prior abstract principles. The word was originated by the American philosopher, C. S. Peirce, who conceived it as a theory of meaning, but borrowed by William James and John Dewey and converted into a theory of truth.

RATIONALISM

The belief that reason or abstract thought is the prime source of genuine knowledge, and that reason must be the final judge of all statements. Aristotle and the medieval scholastics represent the archetypes of this viewpoint.

RELATIVISM
The doctrine that objects may be defined only by relation to other objects, that there are no absolute standards for making value judgments, and that "truth" is a subjective matter, depending upon the relationship of subject and object.

YIN AND YANG
The two antipodal cosmic principles in Chinese dualistic philosophy: Yin embodies the passive, female element or force, while Yang embodies the active, male element or force. (This duality, however, is often treated as a necessary polarity, with the elements cooperating rather than contending.)

Selected Bibliography

Bakan, David. *The Duality of Human Existence.* Boston: Beacon Press, 1966.

Bateson, Gregory. *Steps to an Ecology of Mind.* New York: Ballantine, 1972.

Berdyaev, Nicolas. *The Fate of Man in the Modern World.* Ann Arbor: University of Michigan Press, 1961.

Berdyaev, Nicolas. *The Meaning of the Creative Act.* New York: Collier Books, 1962.

Buber, Martin. *Between Man and Man.* Boston: Beacon Press, 1955.

Buber, Martin. *Good and Evil.* New York: Scribner, 1952.

Buber, Martin. *I and Thou.* New York: Scribner, 1958.

Bultman, Rudolph. *Existence and Faith.* New York: Meridian Books, 1960.

Burckhardt, Jacob. *Force and Freedom.* New York: Meridian Books, 1955.

Cohen, Morris. *Reason and Nature.* New York: Harcourt, Brace, 1931.

Collingwood, R. G. *The Idea of Nature.* New York: Galaxy Books, 1960.

Friedman, Maurice S. *Martin Buber.* Chicago: University of Chicago Press, 1955.

Friedman, Maurice S. (edit.) *The Worlds of Existentialism*. New York: Random House, 1964.

Hartman, Robert S. *The Structure of Value*. Carbondale: Southern Illinois University Press, 1967.

Hartnack, Justus. *Wittgenstein and Modern Philosophy*. New York: Doubleday, 1965.

Heinemann, F. H. (edit.) *Existentialism and the Modern Predicament*. New York: Harper Torchbook, 1965.

Jeffreys, M. V. C. *Personal Values in the Modern World*. Gretna, La.: Pelican Publishing Co., 1962.

Koch, Adrienne. *Philosophy for a Time of Crisis*. New York: Dutton, 1959.

Kwant, Remy C. *From Phenomenology to Metaphysics*. Pittsburgh: Duquesne University Press, 1966.

Kwant, Remy C. *Phenomenology of Language*. Pittsburgh: Duquesne University Press, 1965.

Laing, R. D. and Cooper, D. G. *Reason and Violence*. New York: Vintage Books, 1971.

Lee, Edward N. and Mandelbaum, Maurice. *Phenomenology and Existentialism*. Baltimore: Johns Hopkins Press, 1967.

Luijpen, William A. *Phenomenology of Natural Law*. Pittsburgh: Duquesne University Press, 1967.

Maritain, Jacques. *Existence and the Existent*. New York: Vintage, 1966.

Maslow, Abraham H. (edit.) *New Knowledge in Human Values*. New York: Harper & Row, 1959.

Maslow, Abraham H. *Toward a Psychology of Being*. New York: Van Nostrand Reinhold, 1962.

Merton, Thomas. *Faith and Violence*. Notre Dame: University of Notre Dame Press, 1968.

Morgan, George W. *The Human Predicament*. Providence: Brown University Press, 1968.

Mounier, Emmanuel. *Be Not Afraid*. New York: Harper & Row, 1948.

Mounier, Emmanuel. *Personalism*. London: Routledge & Kegan, 1952.

Mounier, Emmanuel. *The Character of Man*. New York: Harper & Row, 1949.

Norris, Louis W. *Polarity*. Chicago: Regnery, 1956.

Northrop, F. S. C. *The Logic of the Sciences and the Humanities*. New York: Macmillan, 1947.

Northrop, F. S. C. *Man, Nature and God.* New York: Simon & Schuster, 1962.

Nucho, Fuad. *Berdyaev's Philosophy: The Existential Paradox of Freedom and Necessity.* New York: Doubleday, 1966.

Olson, Robert G. *An Introduction to Existentialism.* New York: Dover, 1962.

Pitcher, George (edit.). *Wittgenstein: The Philosophical Investigations.* New York: Doubleday, 1966.

Polanyi, Michael. *Personal Knowledge.* New York: Harper Torchbook, 1964.

Rome, Sydney & Beatrice (edit.). *Philosophical Interrogations.* New York: Holt, Rinehart & Winston, 1964.

Sadler, William A. *Existence and Love.* New York: Scribners, 1969.

Sorokin, P. A. *The Crisis of Our Age.* New York: Dutton, 1941.

Takmon, J. L. *The Unique and the Universal.* London: Secker & Warburg, 1965.

Thorpe, W. H. *Science, Man and Morals.* Ithaca: Cornell University Press, 1965.

Tillich, Paul. *My Search for Absolutes.* New York: Simon & Schuster, 1967.

Weisskopf, Walter A. *Alienation and Economics.* New York: Dutton, 1971.

Whitehead, Alfred North. *Process and Reality*. New York: Macmillan, 1929.

Whitehead, Alfred North. *The Function of Reason*. Boston: Beacon Press, 1959.

Wiener, Philip P. (edit.). *Values in a Universe of Change*. New York: Doubleday, 1958.

Zaner, Richard M. *The Way of Phenomenology*. New York: Pegasus, 1970.